IDAHO
BEER

IDAHO
BEER

FROM GRAIN TO GLASS
IN THE GEM STATE

STEVEN J. KOONCE
FOREWORD BY GREG KOCH

AMERICAN PALATE

Published by American Palate
A Division of The History Press
Charleston, SC 29403
www.historypress.net

Cover photo by Carol M. Highsmith, courtesy of the Library of Congress Carol M. Highsmith Archive.

Images courtesy of author unless otherwise noted.

First published 2014

Manufactured in the United States

ISBN 978.1.62619.379.6

Library of Congress CIP data applied for.

This book is dedicated to the creative men and women in America's craft beer industry, as well as to my lovely bride-to-be, Valerie, without whom there would be no book.

CONTENTS

Contents

FOREWORD

B eer: Mundane. Magical. Boring. Bold. Simple. Sublime. Meh. Satisfying. Vacuous. Intense. International. Regional. Commodity. Artisanal. Take your pick; they're all out there.

The generations that have grown up knowing no other world than the one in which computers and iPhones are ever at their fingertips are known as "digital natives." I didn't get my first Mac, a MacPlus, until I graduated from college in 1987. In my day, you had to go to this thing called a "library" (which, admittedly, I rarely did) or the video game arcade (or the entry area at the small-town grocery store, as I did, where I dropped many a quarter pounding the "Fire" button and jamming the joystick, and my wrists, playing *Galaga*). You kids these days don't know how easy you've got it with all of your search engines and game consoles and such.

Also in 1987, I had my very first "real" beer. It was an Anchor Steam. I knew only one place to get it on tap. A little dive punk artists' bar called Al's Bar in downtown Los Angeles. That was it. I never saw it in the stores. The most interesting thing I could find was a big German import brand (that I later learned wasn't even available in Germany, as it was brewed specifically for the gullible American market) with the word "Dark" appended to it, courtesy of the marketing department and some brewing tricks to add color without the bothersome encumbrance of the flavor associated with actually using roasted malts.

If you've matriculated to drinking age anytime in the last twenty years, but especially in the last ten, you're craft beer natives. You kids these days don't know how easy you've got it with your multi-tap craft beer bars and countless hundreds of lineal feet of beer selection at your local markets and bottle shops. Show some respect or get offa mah lawn!

Actually, it's quite a beautiful thing to be a "craft beer native." I'd be lying if some part of me didn't feel just a wee bit jealous. Fortunately, you don't need to worry about me. Not that you were. And you don't need to worry about your own choices. Not that it would occur to you to do so.

Choice. It's that magic word that we often think we have when we actually don't. Particularly when you put the word "free" in front of it. It can be elusive and often quite misunderstood. Take, for instance, the person at the store whom you witness picking up the six'er of the fake "craft" wit beer that's actually made by the large industrial brewer. Is she utilizing free choice? Only, perhaps, the sort that's found on the other end of highly engineered focus groups, somewhat deceptive marketing and advertising campaigns and wholesaler and retailer incentives. If you were able to see it from the inside, you might find it quite insidious. I have, and I do.

Fortunately, however, my dear friends, you have *real* choice in the great state of Idaho—not just the stuff of marketing departments, but the liquid goodness of the craft brewers, within your very own state.

Now, I'm well known for being a bit of a cantankerously outspoken craft beer zealot. Ever since I discovered that there was such an actual thing as "real" beer, I haven't looked back. And I've also been "that guy" next to countless people who've had the great misfortune to sit next to me on a barstool and order up something that demonstrated that they were only employing the illusion of free choice rather than actual real free choice. Yes, a simple beer decision can indeed offer up such insights. True, today some folks find it a delight to learn who this guy is next to them on the barstool, but that's only in more recent years. I still have more years when people thought I was nothing more than an over-opinionated crank. Actually, just this last week, I encountered someone who felt that way. Or perhaps more accurately, he encountered me.

No matter. The point I was so roundaboutly making was…well, I forgot actually. Such is the risk of going off on a tangent while sitting on a barstool. Or anywhere, pretty much, when the half-drained but quite nicely laced second pint is in hand.

Ah yes. I remember. I was talking about how you kids these days have it so great, but all the while the marketing departments at big corps are still successfully creating obfuscating brands that fool kind folk into making what they think is a choice of free will, as well as that in the beautiful

Greg Koch, co-founder and CEO of Stone Brewing Company. *Courtesy Stone Brewing Company.*

state of Idaho, there are actual, real, honest-to-goodness, full-of-awesomeness choices for you that are produced by passionate artisanal brewers who are quite deserving of your attention. I might not have fully made that last point before trailing off previously, but I have now. And I'll stick by it.

Make no mistake: I love the fact that my beer is one of the quality choices you have to choose from in your local purveyor of finer libations. However, this is a book about Idaho craft beer, not some zealotry-driven cantankerous get-offa-mah-lawn craft brewer from San Diego. (The last part is a bit of a joke, however, as I don't really have a lawn, seeing as how San Diego is pretty much a desert climate and I prefer to save my water for drinking, making beer and, I suppose, the occasional Sunday bath.)

So, dear friends, I'd like to close by pointing out that free choice is most easily made with the help of friends. Friends, and even the cantankerous zealot whom you may find you had the good fortune to sit next to at the bar, can help us to make informed, quality decisions. This here book in your hands is just such a friend. The more time you spend with it, the more you have the opportunity to soak up its wisdom and maybe, just maybe, go down your own road of joyful, informed and passionate zealotry.

And speaking of the zealot, next time you're bellied up to your favorite bar, look into the mirror on the back bar, and you might even find one day that he's sitting on your barstool. I hope I get a chance to sit next to you someday. Honestly, I think zealots, especially craft beer zealots, can be quite fun to while away a pint with.

GREG KOCH
Co-Founder, Stone Brewing Company

ACKNOWLEDGEMENTS

A deeply heartfelt thank-you to my lovely bride-to-be. Valerie. and my soon-to-be stepchildren, Cameron and Lily, for their support and encouragement in getting me to finish this book. Valerie, in particular, has never stopped encouraging me and believing in me from the moment the publisher offered me the chance to do this project. She has been my biggest cheerleader and best asset during this process, and I could not have done it without her.

A huge thank-you to my parents, Jim and Shannon Koonce, for supporting me from the time that I eschewed law school to go to film school and everything since. Thanks to my brother, Matthew, and his girlfriend, Victoria, for being such great sports as I bullied them into home-brewing and continue to tell them where, and what, to drink up in Seattle.

A big thank-you to Steve, Erin, Hayden and Haddie McCandless for giving me a place to stay in Boise and to Aunt Marlis and Uncle Jim for letting me stay at their house in McCall. Balloon parties and Saturday football are always more fun with somebody.

The photos in this book would not have been possible without Joy Pruitt letting me borrow her beautiful Canon DSLR over and over again. Thank you so much, Joy!

Thanks to Virginia Hutchins and everybody at the *Times-News* for giving me an outlet and a place to find my voice that eventually became this book. I couldn't have done this without that space on magicvalley.com.

Thanks to Dave Cole, Peter Erickson, Kevin Crompton and everybody else over at Epic Brewing Company for giving me the opportunity to realize a dream in working at a brewery. My time there taught me more about beer, business and how to succeed than any other job I have ever had.

Thanks to everybody at The History Press, and mostly Will McKay, who has been very patient and fun to work with.

Thanks to Greg Koch for that wonderful evening out in Mission Beach, when I learned that fizzy yellow beer really is for wussies and that craft beer can taste so freaking good. Thanks for writing such an awesome foreword.

Thanks to everybody I interviewed and spoke to about this book. I hope the owners, brewers, employees and fans of Idaho's breweries, bottle shops, ale houses, malting houses and hop farms appreciate my attempt to quantify the emerging Idaho beer scene—especially Tom Ashenbrener and Natalie Steele at Rudy's, who have been huge supporters of the blog and this book.

A big thank-you goes out to my alma mater, Chapman University.

Selfishly, I want to thank those writers who got me to this place. My earliest influences were the late Hunter S. Thompson and Ralph Wiley; I really miss reading them. Tony Kornheiser—before his fingers stopped typing—invented the blog, only he called it a "columnette," and without that format, I wouldn't be writing this book. Charlie Papazian's book *The Complete Joy of Home Brewing* was a huge inspiration to me as a twenty-one-year-old home-brewer and has continued to help me brew delicious beers. Dave Berry, Michael Lewis and Mike Lupica have always been huge inspirations to me for the way they blend humor and thoughtfulness into their work. The "Sports Guy," Bill Simmons, has been a constant read for me since 1999 and has taught me, more than anything else, the virtues of writing in your own voice and succeeding in new mediums.

To the other people who write and speak to the virtues of America's craft beer movement: we are a part of something that is happening, and it is something that is very important. Fight on and have another! Cheers!

INTRODUCTION

While opening up this book for the first time, go ahead and open yourself up a beer. Even better, crack open an Idaho beer and pour it into a glass. Let's say you choose a Sweetgrass American Pale Ale from Grand Teton Brewing in Victor. The beer pours golden with a yellow-orange base, like the fields of barley that dominate southern Idaho's landscape, with a thick white head lacing around the glass. On the nose are notes of freshly mown grass, much like the first whiff you get inside the Gooding Farms drying room, with orange and grapefruit rind and a bit of cracked grain. Citrus flavors and light, bready malts play on the tongue, and the beer finishes clean and refreshing, like so many rivers that flow through the Gem State.

This isn't just another beer from a great brewery; rather, it's a representation of the state itself. Malted barley grown and harvested from the limitless farms stretching across the horizons of southern and eastern Idaho make up the backbone of these beers, while hops grown in the slightly cooler, elevated plains in western Treasure Valley give the beer its character. Finally, brewers born and raised in Idaho bring the best flavors out of those ingredients, relying on a born and bred individual spirit shared by most Idahoans. That same spirit inspired would-be brewers to start making fresh beer in such far-reaching places as Sandpoint, McCall or Twin Falls.

Take a closer look, and you start to understand the culture of Idaho beer. Sandpoint, home to one of Idaho's best ski resorts and countless cabins lined up from the southern shores of Lake Pend Oreille all the way up to Bonners Ferry, is actually a perfect place for Laughing Dog Brewing Company to open up because of the many thirsty campers and tourists. McCall has some of the best skiing, golfing and boating in the state, as well as a town square featuring two excellent breweries. The two brewpubs, McCall Brewing and Salmon River Brewing, make delicious beers in a town of fewer than three thousand full-time citizens; it just stands to reason that many thousands of part-time residents and tourists are in town every weekend to drink up those brews. Von Scheidt Brewing in Twin Falls is currently the only brewery working in the Magic Valley, serving up its amber ale in kegs and bottles along the Snake River from Burley to Hagerman. Even out in the sparsely populated areas of eastern Idaho, breweries dot the map from Victor down I-15 to Pocatello.

The Idaho brewing community is admittedly young. The capital, Boise, has the distinction of being the most isolated population center in the United States. The nearest big cities are Salt Lake to the southeast (340 miles), Reno to the southwest (422 miles), Spokane to the north (425 miles) and Portland to the west (430 miles). It's no wonder so many brewmasters opened up shop in the mining towns of Idaho during the gold rush of the mid- to late 1800s. Before refrigeration, you could not possibly get a beer in the state until these brave pioneers made their way out west with nothing but a sack of grain, some hops, a kettle and a dream.

Fast-forward to the 1980s, when Idaho once again found itself without a package brewery in the state. So, beers from nearby Bend and Portland became Idaho residents' go-to brews. We see today with the large number of English-style pale ales and chewy, piney IPAs the impact that breweries like Deschutes had on would-be Boise brewers. Almost every brewer or brewery owner in Boise points toward Bend, Oregon's most famous brewery as an early inspiration to what they brew today. Why not? Deschutes makes delicious beers, using malted barley and hops found almost exclusively in the Pacific Northwest. A visitor to Boise can be expected to find at least one beer in any of the many brewpubs or breweries that can be directly linked to a Deschutes product.

When interviewing the brewers, bottle shop owners and other Idaho beer personalities, the brewers and especially the brewery owners would want me to "sample" what they were brewing. Just part of the job, I suppose, and one that I take quite seriously. More often than not, I found myself not just enjoying the beers but *really* enjoying what was in the glass. Every brewery I went to had at least two beers that I thought were great if not excellent. I began to form the opinion that Idaho's beer scene, and Boise's in particular, was enjoying the "calm before the storm" of a burgeoning beer movement akin to Portland in the 1990s. These brewers were all using quality malt, wonderful hops and a wide variety of yeasts to coax out beautiful flavors in their beers. Bar and bottle shop owners were forsaking fizzy yellow beer taps in favor of Salmon River's Udaho Gold or Sockeye's Galena Gold Ales, as well as featuring at least one or two local beers (if not more) on the rest of the taps. What we have going on here is a sapling of a beer scene that will soon grow to be a giant tree. I think you will see why.

Idaho Beer: From Grain to Glass in the Gem State will not be a history of Gem State brewing but rather more like a road map showing where Idaho's great breweries have been and where they are going. The impact of Idaho's agricultural industry cannot be overstated here, with hop and barley farms that go back to the time before Idaho became a state contributing to the history and future of Idaho beers. You will visit some of these farms through this book and see how the knowledge, pride and excitement for what they do has greatly influenced the growth of Idaho's brewing community.

By now, your glass should be just about empty, as mine sadly is, and you're probably staring longingly at your refrigerator, waiting for this to end so you can get a refill. Just remember when you're pouring that Idaho beer into your glass that the golden color, crisp finish and hoppy aromas are most likely products of the whole state and not just where it was brewed. That's what separates Idaho's brewing community from others—our beer is homegrown from grain to glass.

PART I
PLANTING THE SEEDS
FOR IDAHO BEER

TRAILS BLAZED AND BREWERIES RAISED:
A BRIEF HISTORY OF IDAHO BEER

To borrow from the Mel Brooks classic *Spaceballs*, here is the short, short version of the history of Idaho brewing: German and Austrian immigrants came with the miners of the early nineteenth century and set up brewpubs in all the little mining towns in what is now called Idaho. Then, as the mining towns dried up, the breweries went with them. After that, there were a few bigger breweries that did okay but were closed by the early twentieth century. Then Prohibition happened and killed Idaho's brewing industry. There were zero commercial breweries in Idaho from 1960 until 1985.

The bigger story is what's happening now in the Gem State brewing scene, and that started happening when August Busch III, who owns a home in Driggs, decided that he wanted to start using Idaho barley for his Budweiser and Bud Light. According to the Associated Press, Anheuser-Busch has contracted double its needs since 2001. Not only that, but Mexico's biggest brewer, Groupo Modelo, has a malting plant in Idaho Falls along with Anheuser-Busch's plant and the nearby Great Western Malting plant in Pocatello, making eastern Idaho the de facto malting capital in the country.

The oldest picture of downtown Twin Falls, looking down Main Avenue toward Shoshone Street. *Courtesy Tom Ashenbrener.*

The barley industry is important because you don't get the interest or growth in the brewing industry without it. It wasn't until four years after the first barley grain was malted at Great Western Malting that Snake River Brewery opened in Caldwell, Idaho. Two years later, TableRock opened its doors in downtown Boise. Snake River lasted just six years before closing its doors forever, and TableRock nearly went under before being saved and later revived.

To put it in perspective, Boise beers weren't packaged in cans or bottles until Payette Brewing canned its first batch of pale ale in 2011. After TableRock's failed attempt at packaging, the rest of Boise's brewpubs, mainly The Ram, Sockeye and Highlands Hollow, refused to take that big step into packaging.

As Rick Boyd, the owner of Brewforia Beer Market in Meridian, put it, "The only reason Sockeye had interest in growing and building a new brewery and offering cans was because Payette did it. Now it was competition."

Now you have a slew of new Idaho breweries opening up and packaging from day one. Slanted Rock Brewing in Meridian started putting out cans almost as soon as it started brewing. Selkirk Abbey has slowly introduced its bottles into the market with just a handful of beers in twenty-two-ounce bottles being sold in the state. Payette offers four of its beers year round in twelve-ounce cans, while neighbor Crooked Fence has two beers out in cans and several more out in twenty-two-ounce bottles, including seasonal releases.

Laughing Dog Brewing Company, from near Sandpoint, distributes some of its beers in Idaho but has a special deal with big-box liquor store Total Wine & More, putting wonderful Gem State IPAs, stouts and porters into Total Wine stores around the country. McCall Brewing Company has recently started bottling some of its brews in twenty-two-ounce bottles, as has Ketchum's own Sawtooth Brewery. Then, of course, you have Grand Teton Brewing, which has been the most successful of the Idaho breweries to package and sell its beers outside the Gem State.

Idaho's quarter-century drought of commercial brewing success was due to many factors, most notably uneven hop and barley production, as well as the fact that all they produced were German-style light lagers. The seeds of Idaho's burgeoning craft beer movement started as soon as Great Western Malting and other malting plants in eastern Idaho began churning out lightly toasted, fully malted two-row and six-row brewer's malt and wheat. The story continued to develop when hop farmers started to branch out into high-alpha flavoring hops, eschewing nuggets and clusters, which were popular with the lager brewers of the mid-twentieth century. Gooding Farms started to produce Apollo, Bravo, Citra, Centennial and Zeus hops— all big-alpha hops that can be used to bitter or flavor beers. This went hand in hand with the craft beer movement, as more people were demanding big, hoppy IPAs; English-style pale ales; stouts fortified with lots of hops; and piney, resinous American- and English-style barley wines being developed in Portland, Seattle, Colorado and Northern California. It was only a matter of time before Idaho began to get back into the brewing game.

Right now, northern Idaho is home to about a dozen breweries, most of them brewpubs making just enough beer to serve to their patrons. Selkirk Abbey and Laughing Dog Brewing are the two big commercial breweries in the area. Eastern Idaho is home to a few small, local brewpubs that are continuously packed with loyal patrons. Idaho Brewing Company and Snow Eagle Brewing & Grill help keep beer lovers in Idaho Falls from going thirsty, while Portneuf Valley Brewing keeps the Idaho State University beer lovers in Pocatello happy. Bertrum's Brewery and Restaurant continually serves up mouthwatering food with delicious beers. Then, up in the mountains on the Wyoming border, there lie two breweries: Wildlife Brewing and Grand Teton Brewing Company. Victor, Idaho, might be one of the best beer cities in the United States, let alone in Idaho.

The capital of Idaho's brewing community is definitely Boise. Just within the city limits, you will find six breweries or brewpubs. That doesn't even include the three Garden City breweries or the breweries west of town in Meridian and Nampa. Not only that, but more and more bottle shops and alehouses are popping up all around the Treasure Valley. When Brewforia Beer Market opened in 2009, owner Rick Boyd said that it was "the only bottle shop in town." Now, if you go to a Boise-area grocery store, you are just as likely to find twenty-two-ounce bottles of barrel-aged sours as you are to find a pound of ground beef. You can now find six-packs of Outlaw IPA or Sockeye Power House Porter at a local gas station or Crooked Fence Rusty Nail Pale Ale on tap at a sports bar. The craft beer movement that was cultivated down the road in Portland went all the way around the country and finally found the Gem State—maybe, as Boyd put it, because "Boise…was ten to twenty years behind the times."

Farewell Toast for These Breweries

Fun and exciting things are happening right now in the Idaho brewing industry, but you can't make an omelet without breaking a few eggs, and none of the current success stories would have been possible without those breweries that paved the way for the breweries of today.

The current Idaho breweries were not successful overnight. Some that are open today are still making daily efforts to ensure that they are around a month from now. There are a lot of reasons for this. One is that operating a brewery in Idaho is a very expensive prospect, as breweries are taxed at 15 percent per gallon for beers up to 4 percent alcohol by volume and an additional 45 percent for beers over 4 percent; in other words, the beers are taxed the same as wine.

Another big obstacle that Idaho brewers have to overcome is that most Idaho beer drinkers (as in just about every state) are staunch macro-lager drinkers. This means that they go into the gas station or convenience store, pick up a twelve-pack of their favorite American light lager and go home. You don't find a lot of craft beer bars outside Boise for this reason, and this gives struggling breweries fewer taps to occupy.

"There's a common thread through a lot of our early '90s breweries, and Star Garnet is not immune to it," remembered Dave Krick, owner of Bittercreek Alehouse in Boise. "Competing with some of the better regional breweries—the Deschutes, Sierra Nevada, Widmer—it was hard for them to compete. Most restaurants didn't have that many tap handles; they'd have four or five beers on tap, and three of them would be some macros."

CLOSED IDAHO BREWERIES (SINCE 1985)

Brewery	Location	Open Dates
Star Garnet Brewery	Boise	1995–1998
Snake River Brewery	Caldwell	1985–1991
Gem State Brewing	Caldwell	1996–2003
T.W. Fishers	Coeur D'Alene	1987–1999
Coeur D'Alene Brewing Company	Coeur D'Alene	1991–2010
Hollister Mountain Brewing Company	Coeur D'Alene	1996–2001
Brownstone Restaurant & Brewhouse	Idaho Falls	1997–2010
Thunder Mountain Brewery	Ketchum	1993–2002
Treaty Grounds Brewpub	Moscow	1998–2003
Bi-Plane Brewing Company	Post Falls	2011–2013
Pend Oreille Brewing Company	Sandpoint	1996–2003
Muggers Brewpub	Twin Falls	1996–2003
Trail Creek Brewing Company	Twin Falls	2004–2009

List partially gathered from http://mariah95.com/BEER/IdahoBreweries.htm.

Krick, talking about one of Boise's first breweries—Star Garnet—and the other closed breweries, says they had "one common thread. All of them ended up collapsing and then being owned by subsequently whoever owned the property. Star Garnet didn't have that; they just collapsed."

One building in Twin Falls, at 516 Hansen Street South, has housed a failed brewery not once but twice. It was once home to Muggers Brewpub, which Natalie Steele, of Rudy's A Cook's Paradise, said failed because it sold too much booze. "Muggers was a brewery that Twin Falls had for a long time that did super fantastic until it got a liquor license," said Steele. "When I turned twenty-one, it was a hot spot. They got their liquor license, and soon after they weren't there anymore."

After Muggers moved out, Trail Creek Brewing Company opened up, originally to great acclaim. Steele actually worked at Trail Creek when it opened in 2005. "Eric Buehner, from Utah, was the brewer. Eric made great beers, and it was pretty cool. I enjoyed working there and I learned a lot, [but] things just didn't work out."

All we really know is what's going on right now—a craft beer market is emerging in a state that can grow its own barley and hops and has a water table in some parts that mimics the best of Germany. What we know for sure is that great beers are coming out right now, and the brewers who are making them are excited to be a part of this growing market because they have been anticipating this growth. Business owners who struggled during the tough times of the late 2000s are optimistic about a future where they see more black numbers instead of red.

The reason we start with the present is because the number of quality beers and breweries is about to double. In 2014, eight more breweries are due to open and begin making beer in the Boise area (with a ninth tap house opening in northern resort town Hayden). The story of beer in Idaho didn't happen in the '80s, '90s or 2000s—it's happening right now! And Idahoans are very excited.

IT ALL STARTS IN THE GROUND

Southern Idaho, from Blackfoot over to Burley, happens to have the perfect weather and soil conditions to grow barley. The barley that makes its way from the fields to the malting plants has a short way to travel, meaning less time for infestation or spoilage. At Great Western Malting, arguably the two most important people in the building—the plant manager and maintenance manager—have both been there since the plant opened in 1981, meaning that not only does the country's best barley go into the plant, but also, once its there, it's malted by experts in the field.

Agriculture is still Idaho's biggest industry, and the brewing industry has been a boon for Idaho farmers. As soon as Great Western Malting and Anheuser-Busch began contracting more and more farmers, barley suddenly became a cash crop for hundreds of thousands of acres of farms. Anheuser-Busch isn't going to slow down production of Bud Light anytime soon, and with the craft beer movement hitting the Gem State, barley farmers in Idaho have a bright future ahead of them.

Two long trellises of Bravo hops waiting to be harvested at Gooding Farms in Parma.

The Body and Soul of Beer: Malted Grain

The three biggest barley-producing states, in no particular order, are Montana, North Dakota and Idaho. But no other state produces two-row brewer's barley for malting right now like Idaho. North Dakota's fields are better suited for six-row barley, and the yields coming out of that state are far less than the yields seen in the Gem State.

Idaho's barley-growing region is considered to be a high desert region. The barley that comes from these high desert farms has an acceptance rate between 95 and 100 percent.

The acceptance rate of barley is the amount of grain grown that is malted and used to brew beer. Low acceptance rates can be due to infestation of bugs or disease, broken skins on the malt or high moisture

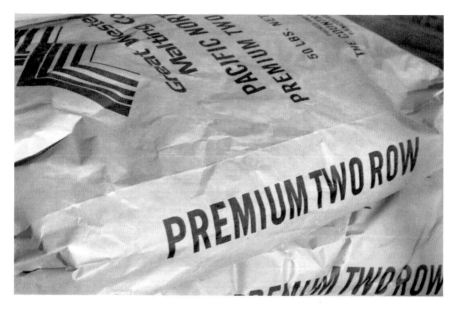

A sack of premium two-row malt from Great Western Malting.

in the kernels. When acceptance rates are up, it means bigger profits for both farmers and the malting plant. Idaho's farms get 95 percent of grain through the malting process, while other states, like North Dakota, only get about 55 percent through on average, meaning that Idaho farms are much more economical and profitable, thus making Idaho one of the nation's best barley-producing states.

Randy Neiwirth of Great Western Malting boiled down Idaho's success in barley production the best: "Consistent production, low humidity, irrigation. Growers are willing to learn and do things right and produce product that we like. It's been a profitable crop for them, and they're doing a great job."

Being part of the barley procurement team means having to work with a lot of farmers. The two-man team of Clay Kaasa and Randy Neiwirth has more than fifty years' combined experience procuring barley for Great Western Malting. Randy Neiwirth started with Great Western in 1975 after graduating from Idaho State University with a degree in crop and soil technology and a brief stint working in Nevada. A friend of his got him an interview, and the rest is history. Clay Kaasa has a similar background. After graduating from Montana State University, he went to work for Great

Western Malting in Montana. Now this team manages twenty-five thousand acres of barley in southern Idaho. This means that these two guys are working with up to two hundred farmers, either directly or indirectly, to produce some of the best barley in the country.

There are about 600,000 acres of barley farms across the state of Idaho, and 85 percent of those fields are in southern Idaho. Great Western Malting contracts out 25,000 acres of barley. Those acres account for fifty thousand tons of grain malted per year. Clay and Randy's main job is to be sure that there is always enough grain to keep the machines at the plant going.

The evolution of barley that has allowed craft brewers and home-brewers to produce consistently fantastic beers ironically has its roots in the big macro-breweries against which they fight so hard. The money that big breweries like Anheuser-Busch and MillerCoors pump into the research and development of better grains has allowed for the development of bigger barley kernels that get better yields and better acceptance rates than the Klages grains that were used in the '70s and '80s.

Two-row grain grown today, compared to the old Klages varieties, has a much bigger kernel size, which means more brewing sugars per pound than smaller two- and six-row breeds. These new grains bring with them better extract rates as well, which basically means that you need less grain to produce a 5 percent beer now then you did even ten or fifteen years ago. It's no accident that Idaho grains have gotten better with time; these new varieties have been bred for success.

The extraction rate or "extract" of the grain is the amount of sugar that can be converted from the starch of the grain. When brewers use two-row malt, they want a higher extraction than from six-row malt, where you want a higher diastatic power. The diastatic power refers to the grain's ability to convert starches to simple sugars. Six-row grain brewers usually use adjuncts—rice, corn or wheat—in the mash to create digestible sugars for yeast. Higher diastatic power in grains means better extract from the adjuncts. One reason craft beers tend to cost more than macro-lagers is because of the use of two-row pale base malts and no adjuncts compared to the traditional use of rice and corn in macro-lagers with the cheaper six-row malted barley.

The university breeding program at Aberdeen has been a huge part of the success of Idaho's barley program. Programs like this are funded by the big breweries in order to produce grains that are both more flavorful and convert into better brewing sugars for beer. According to the Idaho Barley Commission, Anheuser-Busch contracts more than 20 million bushels of Idaho grain per year. Augustus Busch III himself said, "Idaho producers have shown us that they take great pride in producing the very best quality malting barley."

The best evidence that can be found about the abundance of quality barley and wheat grown in Idaho are the three malt houses within fifty miles found between Idaho Falls and Pocatello. Those three malting houses, and the beers brewed from them, are a testament to the quality and quantity of grain found in the Gem State.

MillerCoors has been contracting barley in Idaho for more than forty years. It developed and exclusively grows proprietary versions of Moravian, a two-row barley developed and grown in and around Burley just for MillerCoors products. MillerCoors also operates its own development program in Burley and a storage site in Buhl.

That's not all. Groupo Modelo, now owned by Anheuser-Busch parent company InBev, built its own malting facility in Idaho Falls in 2005 that is operated by worldwide food conglomerate Cargill. Groupo Modelo commands 61 percent market share of Mexico beer, with its biggest brand, Corona, commanding 28 percent of the American market. The Modelo plant produces 7 million pounds of malt per week, which comes out to 182,000 tons of malt per year.

A Tour of Great Western Malting

The Great Western Malting plant in Pocatello produced its first piece of malt in September 1981, and it was Klages. Since then, the plant has turned out ninety-five thousand tons of malt per year. If you put all of that malt into rail cars and stretched it out, the train would cover sixteen miles of track.

The first thing you notice is just how massive the plant itself is from up close. When looking at the building, you notice that it is separated into two halves: germination and kilning. Each half is divided into a dozen floors, and each floor has a purpose. The Great Western Malting plant can separate, steep and dry up to three batches at a time.

Great Western Malting in Pocatello.

"Quality," "consistency" and "safety" are words that aren't just thrown around Great Western Malting. Each and every train car and truck is thoroughly checked for impurities, imperfections and infections. If protein and moisture specs taken from a sample of any of those cars or trucks don't meet the criteria set by Great Western's clients, then the whole truck or car is dismissed. The barley is unloaded into two giant elevators and run to the top of the warehouse. It then passes through a series of gates on its way to a separator, which takes away all the wheat, oats and other impurities that may have been in the car or truck, as well as the straw and thistle that made their way into the shipment from the kernels of barley. The barley is also graded because different customers like different sizes of barley for their mix.

Customer care, along with safety and quality, is a big part of what Great Western Malting does. Plant Manager Tevis Vance put it best: "We pride ourselves on taking care of the customer. Whether it's Penny [Pink, owner of Portneuf Valley Brewing] getting her couple of thousand pounds of malt, we put her blends together the same as if somebody is buying eighty thousand from us. We're customer-driven. In my opinion, that's an Idaho attitude."

The grain then goes into steeping vessels, which are lined up on an entire floor like a series of pods on an alien spaceship. The barley is steeped in a giant, conical tank that circulates air and heated water through the kernels. The barley stays in the steeping tank for about two days. Great Western can steep 230 tons of barley at once.

> *The steeping tank is one of the coolest pieces of equipment in the entire malting plant. It's shaped like a big cone, with a valved bottom and a grated cone that moves oxygen and carbon dioxide through the grain while it sits in circulating water. The air and water temperature and CO_2 levels are controlled by computer that can be accessed at a terminal near the steeping tanks, in the office and on the home computers of Plant Manager Tevis Vance, as well as the Maintenance Manager, Steve Brammer.*

The grains are put into a germination bed, where they germinate for up to four days. This not only changes the exterior of the grain, causing the addition of sprouts onto the kernel, but it also dramatically changes the interior, where once useless starches begin to turn into wonderful digestive sugars for the yeast. This is basically the malting process: turning starches inside the grain into sugars used for brewing beer. The germination period is the most important part of the malting process and determines the extract rate of the grain.

Next, the grain is taken to the kiln phase. Exactly what it sounds like, the kiln process roasts the grains, halting the growing process and creating a little bit of crunch on the outside of the grain to give it that extra flavor. Great Western Malting uses a two-kiln process. The first phase brings the moisture of the grain from 45 percent down to just 18 percent. The next phase brings that number down to 4 percent moisture and gives the grain a light roast. Each kiln requires you to go through an airlock to get into, where you are immediately greeted by the sweet, roasty smell of lightly toasted malt. Kilning typically takes about one and a half days.

Tevis Vance, plant manager at Great Western Malting, has been at the plant since before the beginning and takes great pride in the malt he produces, as well as the people who help produce it. "The people raising the barley are people from our community. The people that are making the malt are people from Idaho. The people that are brewing the beer are just people from here in Idaho. There's something to be said for that. We're just really fortunate to be located in an area where the quality of the barley and quality of the malt and quality of the customers are just such high quality."

Great Western Malting has become a huge advocate for craft beer. "Growth in the beer business is growth for the malt business," noted Vance about the multitude of new breweries. "Their growth is very exciting for us. We have programs to help them with storage; we have dedicated trailers to haul their malt. We think it's a great part of our business."

It goes both ways. Great Western Malting and subsidiary Country Malt are the overwhelming favorites for base malts across Idaho. Grand Teton, Sockeye Brewing, Payette and others have silos that receive 100 percent Idaho-grown malted barley from Great Western Malting. "All of our two-row malt comes from Idaho," said Max Shaffer of Grand Teton Brewing.

"Idaho is a great barley-growing region," added Penny Pink, owner of Portneuf Valley Brewing in Pocatello. "We produce some of the best barley in the world, malting barley specifically. It's why Budweiser has a plant here." Not coincidentally, Penny gets all of her base malt at neighboring Great Western Malting.

"We get all of our base malt and our silo malt right from Pocatello, Idaho, so there's definitely a conscious effort," said TableRock head brewer Derek Anderson about using local grains. "Anytime you can use the ingredients that are indigenous to your area, I think that's something you always strive for."

Malted barley and wheat might be the backbone to any great beer, but Idaho also produces another key component to beer: hops. Or, as Tevis Vance put it, "we picture like if beer is a steak, then malt is the meat and the salt and pepper is the hops."

Gooding Farms and Idaho's Hop Business

Hops are a finicky plant. They are so difficult to cultivate and grow that most varieties of them can be grown only along the 49th parallel north—not just in the United States but in the world. Even when you happen to have some land on that parallel, it doesn't necessarily mean that you can just put up a hop farm. If the weather is a little too warm or too humid, then certain varieties just won't grow, yet other varieties will grow in abundance in that same weather. Hops are finicky.

"We don't get too much hail or adverse weather conditions that could be potentially crop threatening," said Dianne Haas of Gooding Farms. "We're at the right latitude. Hops are very daylight-sensitive."

A sign at Gooding Farms in Parma.

Hops are divided into two distinct varieties: alphas and aromas. Alphas, which refer to alpha acids in the hop oils, are used primarily for bittering beers, while aroma hops are used to add hop aromas and flavors into the beers. Breeds derived from classic noble hops used for bittering light lagers were once the only hops grown in Idaho, and they were grown for macro-breweries like Anheuser-Busch and Coors. These hops still account for the largest number of breeds grown in the Gem State.

Growers in the western Treasure Valley started out growing nothing but Cluster hops. Clusters are the oldest variety of United States–bred hops. These hops were perfect for bittering any type of beer and were widely used for that purpose.

Mike Gooding's family has been growing hops since the late 1800s, and with his daughter, Dianne Haas, involved in the family farm, they will continue to grow hops into the future. His family started growing hops in Oregon in 1888. It wasn't until 1931 that his grandfather's cousin started growing hops in Idaho. "My grandfather had been through this valley in 1931, and he liked how dry it was," recalled Mike Gooding. "He liked the fact that there was irrigation, and he said if [he] ever got a chance to grow hops here, [he would]."

That chance ended up happening when Gooding's grandfather bought out his cousin, and Gooding Farms was born. Gooding Farms, like Elk Mountain Farms outside Bonners Ferry, started out growing mainly alpha hops for macro-lagers. As the times have changed, however, Gooding Farms has been able to expand to some really great new varieties of hops that have high alpha acid levels in addition to properties found in popular aroma hops.

"We do real well with Zeus. We do as good or better than the Yakima Valley. Apollo, Bravo, maybe just as good," noted Gooding about the new varieties that he's producing now. "And then on the aroma side, we can grow Cascades and Chinooks very well here."

Dianne doesn't shy away when asked about Idaho's hops compared to Oregon or Washington's vaunted farms. "We hold our own as far as oil properties and characteristics go, as well as yields per acre. We're very comparable; we're just in a different area."

The life of a hop starts in February, when Gooding's workers get out and start digging roots. A quick start means better yield from the crop. Gooding noted that they "dug and planted [the Cluster hops] *before the end of February, and those root planted Cluster babies went over ten bales an acre. They were outstanding and exceptional." The longer you wait, the fewer yields you're going to get.*

Gooding Farms has been able to grow as many as a dozen different hop varieties for commercial use. Those varieties include the aforementioned Apollo, Bravo, Zeus, Cluster, Cascade and Centennial along with Citra, CTZ (a hybrid of Columbus, Tomahawk and Zeus breeds), El Dorado and Chinook, among others. These represent the growing interest in flavor hops—and hoppy IPAs—not only from Idaho breweries but also from around the country.

"Market demands," as Mike Gooding explained about the rise of aroma hop varieties on his farm, "…they usually require changing varieties before anything else does. Sometimes we get one that's a poor yielder, and we'll pull it out, but most of the time, it's market conditions. You know, we were growing alphas here almost exclusively for the last ten or fifteen years, and

Hops are taken from the field and harvested using a pulley system that takes the hops up into a separator before being dried.

then all of a sudden, with craft brewing, with their rise to prominence, the aromas have taken front and center stage."

The aromas in question that have come to prominence around the country are represented at Gooding Farms. Citra, Centennial and Cascade hops are perhaps the most sought-after aroma hop varieties this side of Simcoe.

Many brewers like to put out a fresh hop, or harvest, ale during the hop harvest. Using wet, or un-dried, hops allows brewers to put something different out during the fall months and gives them a reason to head out to a farm and pick some hops. Two talented brewers—Shawn Kelso from 10 Barrel and Mike Francis from Payette—use Gooding Farms hops to brew some beautiful, fresh hop beers.

Two excellent harvest ales produced from Gooding Farms hops came from two of the best breweries in Idaho: Payette Brewing and 10 Barrel Brewpub. Payette made two fresh hop beers: Wet and Wilder and So

Fresh & So Clean. Wet and Wilder is a really clean, flavorful IPA with sweet grapefruit flavors derived from fresh Chinook hops harvested and brought directly to Payette. 10 Barrel's Big Daddy Fresh Ale is a fantastic harvest ale created with Cascade hops, also picked at Gooding Farms. "Big Daddy" refers to Mike Gooding. About the fresh hop harvest, Gooding said, "It's a fun day. They get green hops, and they brew them. It's fun for them, and it's fun for us. They almost always make sure we get a sample or two back."

Goose Island, which uses hops exclusively from Elk Mountain Farms outside Bonners Ferry, released a pale ale called 10 Hills Pale Ale to celebrate the original ten hills of hops with which it started out at Elk Mountain. Now that brewery uses more than 200,000 bushels of Idaho hops per year.

One thing about hop farming, besides having to deal with finicky hops and a small window for planting and harvesting, is that it's very expensive. Most farms require some dirt, a hole in the ground and water. Hop farming requires an intricate trellis and cable system to maximize the amount of hops you can grow on each acre.

The economics of farming are always a big topic of interest in Idaho, but in this case, it could mean the difference between an emerging source of income or maintaining the status quo. Presently, Idaho stands at only 15 percent of the nation's hop market. With two distinct growing regions, more craft breweries and a growing interest in locally sourced material, it isn't too hard to imagine that number going up.

The growing interests of local brewers to source their hops locally is a huge part of taking market share away from the Yakima and Willamette Valleys. "Southern Idaho hops are among the best I've ever used," said Rob Mullin, brewmaster of Grand Teton Brewing. "Currently, Idaho hops account for about half of our usage. We expect them to be about 85 percent of our total by the end of our current five-year contracting period."

Grand Teton, perhaps the state's biggest production brewery, has switched out English hop varieties for hops grown in southern Idaho in its longstanding Teton Ale. Bitch Creek and 208 Session Ale are brewed with large amounts of Idaho-bred hops (208 Session Ale exclusively uses Idaho-grown hops).

Idaho beer lovers can take pride the next time they sit down to drink a locally produced beer, knowing that the meat of the beer—and maybe the seasoning as well—is most likely grown and produced right here in the Gem State.

PART II
RESTARTING IDAHO'S BREWING TRADITION

IT CAME FROM THE TETONS

As I made my way through the icy, twisting roads of Targhee National Forest, my only thought was, "Don't die." What I found waiting for me was a gorgeous canyon separating Idaho from Wyoming and containing arguably the best brewery in Idaho: Grand Teton Brewing.

When it isn't the middle of winter, I imagine that the drive from Idaho Falls to Victor would be quite beautiful and relaxing. In between the two mountain passes, you travel past a gorgeous lake, with a river that leads you up to Targhee National Forest. Targhee, as it's known throughout the Mountain West, is one of the best ski hills you will find anywhere in the Rockies. Just before you reach Jackson Hole, Wyoming, you come upon the small (there's literally one stoplight) town of Victor, which is home to two breweries: Grand Teton and Wildlife Brewing. Grand Teton no longer relies on just tourism to sell its beer; now it distributes to fifteen states. You can find multi-gold-medal-winner Bitch Creek ESB on tap or in bottles in California, Washington, Nevada, Montana, Wyoming, Colorado, Kansas, Missouri, South Carolina, Illinois, Wisconsin, Minnesota and both Dakotas. No other brewery in Idaho has as much national exposure, and no other brewery in Idaho is as difficult to reach.

It is one reason I risked my life (and that of my truck's) to slip and slide down Targhee National Forest's roads to meet with what many consider to be the best production brewery in Idaho and to discover what makes Grand Teton beer so damn good.

A Beginning: Otto Brothers' Brewing

Grand Teton started in Wyoming as the Otto Brothers' Brewing Company. Founded by Charlie and Ernie Otto in 1988, it was the first "micro" brewery in the state of Wyoming. The Otto brothers, who came from German-Austrian descent, wanted to make fresh, full-flavored, locally brewed beers and found the waters coming off the Tetons to be the perfect place to start. They actually picked up the first malt beverage manufacturing permit in Wyoming in more than three decades. It was in this small brew house that they first made "Teton Ale," a wonderful amber-style beer that was considered pretty bold in the macro-dominated '80s, and history was made. Soon, taps all over Jackson Hole were dominated by Teton Ale, Old Faithful Ale and Moose Juice Stout, as happy skiers and vacationers were treated to some of the best beer in the country.

The brothers also made a fairly significant rediscovery when they introduced a sixty-four-ounce glass container that people could fill up and take home called a "growler." Otto Brothers' Brewing Company was indeed the brewery to introduce this handy and environmentally friendly way to transport fresh draft beer from your favorite brewpub to the comforts of your home. Raise a glass for the Ottos next time you take a growler home!

The continued growth and popularity of Otto's beers saw the groundbreaking of the current facility in Victor in 1998. In just nine years, Otto Brothers' Brewing had gone from a tiny, self-distributing brewery to the state's first brewpub to breaking ground on a huge production brewery.

Victor, Idaho, was a perfect place for the brewery, with locally sourced grain and hops nearby, as well as the thousands of tourists who would come in (and bring beer back to their homes) to ski at Jackson Hole and Targhee. This beautiful valley also boasts some of the best water for making beer, as it shares characteristics with Munich's drinking water. The water is so good that Grand Teton doesn't alter the chemistry of the ground water at all to make its delicious beers.

The new brewery was able to produce ten thousand barrels annually with the ability to ferment both lagers and ales. It would also house a twelve-

Grand Teton's crew (minus Brewmaster Rob Mullin). *Left to right*: head cellarman Max Shaffer, head brewer Curtis Rohrbaugh and owners Steve and Ellen Furbacher.

ounce bottling line (to go along with a future 750-milliliter and twenty-two-ounce bottling lines) that would increase the ability to distribute beer outside the state.

In the fall of 2000, Otto Brothers' Brewing Company changed its name to Grand Teton Brewing to allow for a more recognizable name that people would identify with the Teton region. In 2009, another monumental shift occurred for the brewery when Charlie Otto decided to sell Grand Teton Brewing to Steve and Ellen Furbacher.

The Furbachers owned a vacation home in Victor and had moved there to retire. Retirement must not have suited them because they purchased the brewery in order to have something to do in retirement and to have something to pass on to their children. They quickly established new long-term goals for the brewery and have since gone on to accomplish those goals. They have added to the production line with new pieces to increase the amount of beer that Grand Teton can package and sell. They also recently purchased a new 30-barrel brew house from Bell's Brewery in Michigan, along with four brand-new 140-barrel fermenters. Ultimately, the goal of the new ownership is to continue to make delicious beers while allowing the brewers to reach the limitless potential of the brewery. It has been an expensive pursuit, but one that Steve Furbacher believes will mean a profitable and award-winning brewery now and into the future.

Grand Teton Today

Grand Teton Brewing has taken a decidedly different approach from some breweries in the way it packages and maintains quality control in its beers. The only Idaho brewery to employ a full-time quality-control person, as well as a 100 percent full-time employee workforce on the brewery floor, Grand Teton has put its money where its mouth is when attempting to produce the best beer in Idaho. Each and every batch of beer is checked for quality at the microscopic level every single time it is moved. This means that the bottle of Sweatgrass that we shared earlier was checked going into the fermenter, coming out of the fermenter in the brite tank and then again after it was bottled to maintain the quality that Grand Teton expects out of its brews. This type of attention to detail is usually done by big breweries like Stone or Sierra Nevada and hardly ever done by a brewery the size of Grand Teton.

"We've turned the usual small brewery approach to quality 180 degrees," said Brewmaster and Chief Operating Officer Rob Mullin. What he means is that instead of sending beer out to the market and waiting to see if customers send it back, Grand Teton tests its beers for microbial infections and does frequent taste tests to ensure quality in every single bottle. Not a drop of beer leaves the brewery until the quality-control manager signs off.

"If subsequent testing or complaints reveal a problem, then [other breweries] recall the beer, pull it off the shelves," said Mullin. "But you can't get it out of the consumers' refrigerators, and they can't un-drink it, so our focus is on finding problems before the beer leaves the brewery."

Each and every bottle coming out of the Victor brewery is also bottle-conditioned, which is something that was started when the Furbachers took over. This means that the beers are never filtered, fined or otherwise cleared. There are no signs of diatomaceous earth or finings anywhere in the brewery. Instead, Grand Teton cold-crashes each and every batch of beer that it produces, allowing the beer to naturally clear.

Cold crashing is a method used by brewers to bring the suspended yeast in fermenting beer to the bottom of the fermenter by chilling the beer to just above freezing temperatures. This not only clears the beer but

Grand Teton Brewing in Victor, Idaho.

also allows the cellar people to take yeast from that tank and use it on another beer. By not using finings (which are often made from fish gills) to clear beer, craft breweries can also claim to have a vegetarian- or vegan-friendly product.

This is particularly useful when crafting beers that can be aged, as the beer is still technically alive when it comes out of the brewery and will go through subtle changes until the yeast stops creating carbon dioxide, at which point you should drink the beer or suffer the horrible fate of holding on to a beer for too long. Thankfully, Grand Teton's Cellar Reserve beers are each conditioned to last between eight months and three years after the bottling date, which is printed on the 750-milliliter bottle, so you will never suffer from flat, albeit aged, beer.

"I try to keep our beer a couple years," said Rob Mullin. "Problem is, I never make it; I drink them before they age!"

The changes in Grand Teton Brewing are really starting to show in the beers that it produces. It is now able to produce six full-time beers to go along with a full year of seasonal offerings and the Cellar Reserve series to show off what that new thirty-barrel brew house can really do. The six year-long "Signature Brews" include Teton Ale, Bitch Creek ESB, Sweetgrass American Pale Ale, Howling Wolf Weiss Beer, Old Faithful Ale and the brand-new 208 Session Ale. These beers make up the backbone of Grand Teton and show off exactly what this brewery is all about.

Bitch Creek ESB (Extra Special Brown) was one of the first, if not the first, hoppy brown ales to be produced in the United States. This beer, which has won an astounding ten medals, boasts big nutty flavors with caramel overtones and huge resinous hoppy flavors that finish the beer off nicely. Named after a creek found along the Wyoming-Idaho border, this beer is an adventure unto itself and has spawned a brand-new beer category: Extra Special (or hoppy) Brown.

"We won two golds in a row for it at the Great American Beer Festival," Mullin told me, "which definitely put us on the radar. It was the first beer I formulated from scratch here. It didn't really fit any style guidelines but was instead my attempt to create a truly indigenous Pacific Northwest beer. Untreated Teton Valley water, plenty of malt backbone and two varieties of hops—Chinook and Galena—born here in Idaho."

Sweetgrass American Pale Ale is simply one of the best big pales that can be found in the country, let alone in Idaho. That claim is backed up by a gold medal at the Great American Beer Festival in 2009, and it is one of the bestselling beers in the state. Sweetgrass pours a beautiful golden color, with a sticky white head that laces nicely down the glass. Notes of sweet malt and grassy hops are balanced by citrusy hop flavors and a bitter finish that you don't get in most pale ales. Poured from the tap, the grapefruit and grassy hop aromas hit your olfactory senses before you even see the beer! Sweetgrass was originally listed as an IPA and got no love in competition, so the brewery decided to switch it to the then less-competitive American pale ale category, and it won a gold. Just goes to show that while you shouldn't judge a book by its cover, you can judge a beer by its style.

With apologies to one wonderful brewery in Fort Collins, if Teton Ale were produced at the clip of one very popular, nationally available amber ale, then this would be the standard by which all ambers were judged. Clean and crisp with just a bit of hoppiness and a lot of crystal malt flavor, Teton Ale tastes great after a day of skiing or in the backyard during a barbecue.

American wheat lagers aren't quite as popular or prevalent as other styles, but when one is done right, the flavors of straw and sourness of the wheat play strongly on the palate while also maintaining the refreshing nature of a light lager, and that is just what you get with Howling Wolf,

A true Pacific Northwest beer, Bitch Creek ESB, adorned with its Great American Beer Festival medals.

which is a perfect lawnmower beer that refreshes and has wonderful flavors of hay and sour wheat, as well as a bit of clove from the Bavarian hefeweizen yeast strain used to ferment the beer.

Old Faithful Ale is a pale golden ale that is popular in the region, as you see this type of beer all over Idaho Falls, Targhee and Jackson Hole. It's a nice complement to the hoppy Sweetgrass and bolder Bitch Creek and would be an excellent craft alternative for people who love light American lagers.

That brings us to the uniquely Idahoan 208 Session Ale.

The Story of the 208

The 208 Session Ale, named for the sole area code in the Gem State, came together as a sort of thank-you to Idaho beer drinkers, as well as to the people in Idaho who produce the wonderful barley and hops found in the state. Steve Furbacher and general sales manager Chuck Neuicky had a vision of beer made from ingredients only found in Idaho. It would showcase the two-row malt that Idaho is famous for, along with hops from Idaho's many hop regions.

The first 100 percent Idaho-made beer: 208 Session Ale, made from Idaho hops, barley and water.

"With our 208 Session Ale, we're trying to reach out beyond the typical craft beer drinker to those who buy their beer at the gas station or grocery store," said Brewmaster Rob Mullin. "Through our packaging, we're trying to spread the amazing story of Idaho malt and hops. 208 is the first all-Idaho beer ever bottled, and it's by far our fastest-growing product."

The result is a really nice, drinkable beer with sweet malt flavors and grassy, subtle hop bitterness. The 208 Session Ale is a fantastic bridge beer for people looking to get away from macros and into the wonderful world of craft beer. One of the best parts of 208 is the price point, which is significantly lower than that of other craft beers.

Mullin put it more succinctly. "We really want to be thought of as 'Idaho's Craft Brewery,' the first brewery people think of when they look for beer here."

BIG BEER BUSINESS IN SMALL RESORT TOWNS

Because of where the Gem State is located—with the Rocky Mountains trailing up through the southeast part of the state, the Bitterroot Range curving through the northeast and the Salmon River and Sawtooth Mountains bubbling up in the middle—you can land in any airport in Idaho and be on a ski lift in about an hour, less if you use the regional airports found in second-home havens Hailey and McCall. Not only are these beautiful mountains providing the slope and snow for world-class skiing and snowboarding, but also the resorts built at the bases of the lifts provide fantastic amenities sought out by the world's wealthiest ski bums. Drive into any resort town in Idaho, and you'll first notice the population, normally fewer than 3,500 people, and next you'll notice how many homes, condos and resorts dot the landscape. If you are like me, you will then notice that in towns like McCall, there is a brewery for every 1,000 full-time residents. That's a statistic that I can get behind!

Fishing in Idaho isn't just a sport. It's a way of life. The state's identity is tied to the lure of its clear streams, rivers and lakes so much that we elected a governor with the last name "Otter." One 2005 report completed on the total economic impact of anglers in the state noted that more than $500 million will be spent by anglers before and during their fishing trips to Idaho. It's no wonder that we have breweries with names like Salmon River, Sockeye and Payette or that when Payette and Sockeye decided to package, they went with the river-friendly cans instead of bottles.

Resort towns are perfect places to set up shop if you're a brewery owner trying to reach the masses. People come into your town and try Bitch Creek ESB. They go home to Illinois—with a growler or two—and talk up your brewery with their friends, and before you know it, distributors are calling you up wondering if they can put Bitch Creek on tap at First Draft and

Crooked Pint Ale Houses in Chicago. Now, instead of being a two-thousand-barrel micro-brewery just outside Jackson Hole serving skiers and locals, you are a ten-thousand-barrel-production brewery serving more than a dozen states and markets that have as many residents in one apartment complex as the entire town in which you brew.

It all begins with tourism. The tourism starts with the beautiful makeup of the state—or, as McCall Brewing Company owner Louis Klinge put it while discussing why people come to play in Idaho, "the whole state is a playground for America."

Salmon River Snags a Big One

McCall, Idaho, with a population of about three thousand full-time residents, seems like a wonderful place to go to ski, snowshoe or hike during the winter. But at its heart, McCall is a summer lake town.

"This place blows up to fifteen thousand in the summer, thirty to sixty thousand for Fourth of July," Matt Ganz said with a sparkle in his eye. "This is a lake town. In terms of activity and revenue, it's all about summer."

Matt Ganz and Matt Hurlbutt, the co-founders of Salmon River Brewery, are excited. They are fidgety with nerves because they are about to move into a new brewpub that will, conservatively, triple their current business.

Ganz isn't the nervous type; in fact, he is blatantly fearless. Before taking up the comparatively relaxing profession of co-owning a brewery, he jumped out of planes and fought fires…in Alaska. "I came up here to be a smoke jumper. That's somebody who jumps out of airplanes and manages wildfires," said Ganz, as if he were bagging groceries or dog-walking instead of going headfirst into forest fires.

After a brief foray into spray-foam installation, Ganz decided to get into the old family business of brewing. His maternal family, the Hemmerichs, emigrated from Germany in 1850 and started a brewery in Wisconsin called Alma Brewery. Soon after, the Hemmerichs continued west to Seattle, where they started Bay View Brewing in 1878. This became Seattle Brewing and Malting Company, famous for brewing Rainier Pale, with the big red *R*. By 1884, the name had changed to Rainier Brewing Company, one of the most famous Northwest breweries in history.

"A light bulb went off, and I'm like, 'Why don't I "tap-in" to the old family business!' My wife gave me the green light to follow my dreams," Ganz related. He told his wife, Ellen—a realtor in McCall—his new plans, and she

Salmon River Brewery's new brewpub (presently minus the brewery) on Payette Lake in McCall.

quickly found him a location that would be perfect for his next enterprise. It was across the street from a popular coffeehouse and owned by fellow realtor Jennifer Hurlbutt's husband, Matt, whom they had seen around town and knew socially.

"I got a phone call from Matt. [We] bought that home seven or eight years ago, and we had it as a rental," Hurlbutt recalled. "He wanted to start a micro-brewery in McCall. It took me about five, ten seconds to ask him if he was interested in a partner."

Matt Hurlbutt had home-brewed for close to a decade, but Ganz had never brewed. Hurlbutt was able to get a half-barrel pilot system from a friend, and they were soon coming up with recipes and home-brewing them up as quickly as they could. After a year of fine-tuning their recipes, they secured a loan and bought their first brew house. They picked up a used seven-barrel system along with some open fermenters. They still use that system today but have recently switched to closed fermenters, which save on space.

Salmon River was soon experiencing a boom of its own. That Colorado Street location was packed night in and night out with locals seeking a cool vibe and live music and tourists seeking some fresh beer after a day on the lake. The four staples of Salmon River—Udaho Gold, Quiver IPA, PFD Pale Ale and Buzz Buzz Coffee Porter—could be found in pizza places and restaurants all over the McCall region. Things got so crazy that the two neophyte brewers were having trouble keeping up with demand.

"During the summer, we got down to none of our own beers. We ran out of beer," Hurlbutt explained. "So, we got Payette and Sockeye and Grand Teton and Laughing Dog. We tried to buy all these Idaho beers, and we did this Idaho tap takeover to spin our failure of running out of beer," he noted, laughing. From then on, they decided that the experiments would have to wait while they focused on those core four beers. This would turn out to be a wonderful decision.

Udaho Gold is a wonderful bridge beer for people still stuck on macrobrews. It's a beer for people looking to get into craft beer but not yet ready to hop into the world of imperial stouts and double IPAs. In summation, it's a beer perfect for somebody who is still pining for thirst-quenching lagers but wants a little bit more full-bodied beer with his pizza or burger. A beer like Udaho Gold might even tempt, say, someone whose name is synonymous with American beer. Somebody who comes from the first family of American beer, who just sold his company and is looking for something in which to invest. Somebody like Adolphus Busch IV, of the St. Louis Busches.

"The first time was our first summer. I was there. It was a crazy night. I happened to be working that night in the pub, pouring beer, and we got the word that the Busches were coming in," recalled the exuberant Ganz about the first night Adophus Busch IV walked into Salmon River Brewery.

It all started on a river raft adventure that Busch took with friend of the Matts Dave Bingaman and one of the core four beers, Udaho Gold. "We were out of Gold, man," laughed Ganz. Hurlbutt also began chuckling to himself at the memory. Ganz served him up another Idaho brewery's kölsch-style brews that Busch ended up putting ice cubes in—not a good sign. It's not hard to imagine that Salmon River had just missed out on a monumental opportunity.

"The next summer, I happened to be rolling sushi one lunch, [and] he comes wandering in. He did this like, 'I know you' thing. He kind of looked familiar to me but not really. He's like, 'I met you last summer. My name's Adolphus Busch, and my family just sold our company to InBev,'" Ganz deadpanned about the record-breaking $47 billion takeover that was made on the King of Beers shortly before this meeting. "I said, 'Well, let's get you a beer, what do you want?'" Adolphus ordered an Idaho Gold. Ganz offered him a Udaho

Gold. "So I got him a beer. He drank it and was like, 'Yeah, that's the one.' We talked a little bit more, and he was like, 'I would love to find a way to write up a business plan with you guys and get this beer to St. Louis!'"

Hurlbutt, still laughing to himself, said, "He called me after that, and I was like, 'What? What's going on? Is this *Candid Camera* or something?'"

Adolphus Busch IV is the son of longtime Anheuser-Busch patriarch Augustus "Gussie" Busch Jr. and half-brother to the most recent AB CEO, Augustus Busch III. Adolphus, despite never being involved with Anheuser-Busch, owned Silver Eagle Distributor in Houston, Texas, which is one of the largest beer distributors in the country. He had been coming to McCall for twenty years before going into Salmon River Brewery.

It was no joke. Adolphus Busch IV had basically just offered his assistance to two guys who had started a brewpub in McCall, Idaho—two guys who "ran out of beer" one summer and had to throw a fake beer festival to cover it up. Adolphus Busch IV, who had family pedigree and experience owning successful distributers around the country, would end up paying $300,000 for 49 percent of the company, with a continued interest in Salmon River Brewery. In effect, one of the smallest production breweries in Idaho had just put a member of America's first beer family on its executive board.

Hurlbutt added succinctly, "What that did was it took out our business debt. We were tired of being in debt." Ganz added, "Yeah, our houses were on the line."

The money also allowed them to buy a truck, kegs, tanks, merchandise and some other things that they had wanted to pick up. It also gave them a partner who isn't quite silent but nonetheless has made it clear that he doesn't want to run the company. They also get some unexpected perks, like a full legal team, and the Matts got a little summer help from somebody who might be in their lives for a long time.

"Adolphus asked us if we thought it would be okay if Adolphus V could work in the brewery over this last summer," said Ganz. "We paid him ten dollars an hour, and Matt and I taught Adolphus Busch V how to make beer and clean kegs. It was a trip." Maybe this means that the next generation of Busches will be more focused on craft beer instead of macro-brewed lagers, but who knows.

The Salmon River Matts weren't quite done entertaining offers from wealthy benefactors. Going back to the Colorado Street location for the

Salmon River Brewing's sign in front of its new brewpub in McCall.

brewery, they were never going to be able to become the business they wanted to be while in that small pub. They had created an atmosphere awarded by *The Street* magazine as the best brewpub experience in Idaho. Sitting on the back porch of Salmon River felt like hanging out at a neighbor's backyard but with (mostly) unlimited beer. But there were drawbacks to being just half a block off the main street in what is really a one-street kind of town. As Matt Hurlbutt explained, after five years of business, "We still run into people that have never heard of us and don't know who we are."

Before they could even start looking into moving, an offer came their way from two of the wealthiest landowners in McCall, David and John Cary, who own Hotel McCall and a large chunk of land around Payette Lake. David Cary approached the two and wondered if they would like to move from the Colorado Street location, half a block off the main street and almost a mile from the lake, to the Old Train Depot building, right on the main street overlooking the lake.

The only problem was that Salmon River was built to be a brewpub, first and foremost, and there was no space built that could satisfy the needs of a brewery in or around the Old Train Depot building, in an area known to residents as the Golden Triangle.

"We said, 'We need a brewery.' He said, 'How big?' We came up with doubling our square footage allowing us to double our capacity," Hurlbutt told me, still amazed by his good fortune. "It was flattering for sure. Like, wow, you have this much confidence in us that you're going to build us a two-thousand-square-foot brew house and sign a ten-year lease?"

Of the "core four" beers that Salmon River keeps in the rotation, Buzz Buzz Coffee Porter stands out the most among craft beer fans. The Matts use fair-trade, organic, dark-roasted coffee beans to develop a cold extract from before brewing the beer. The beer itself is a wonderful mix of light chocolate, bitter coffee and roasted caramel malts, leaving the drinker feeling like they just had a caramel macchiato and not an American porter.

The Colorado Street location, which also houses the Hurlbutt family upstairs from the pub, closed on the weekend of Thanksgiving 2013. The brand-new lakefront location opened just a few weeks later, and it has been a wild success. The co-founders have been able to shed many titles from their résumés, including chef, bartender and pub manager, and are now able to concentrate on a brewery's two most important things: customers and beer.

Said Ganz, "We're really going all in on the pub-brewery model. Matt and I are most passionate about crafting beer."

McCall Brewing Company

McCall Brewing Company has had its share of ups and downs over its twenty years of brewing. The brewery, opened in 1994, was a tack shop before being turned into a brewpub. It was bought and sold twice by the original owner, and when current owner Louis Klinge found it, the brewery was bankrupt with a "For Sale" sign in the window. To many, this brewery looked every bit like the bankrupt failure it had come to be, but to Klinge, it represented the chance to fulfill a dream he had since he was a nineteen-year-old college student in Utah.

"I never thought about brewing," started Klinge, smiling a big inviting smile and sipping on one of his signature beers, "until I walked into the Wasatch Brewery in Park City in 1986 and have been planning on owning a brewery since. We walked in and they got all these beers, and we're just standing there with our beer just looking at the tanks and proceeded to drink everything."

Louis soon became the next owner of McCall's oldest brewery. The pub came complete with an eight-barrel system and a brewer, Greg Aimes, who had brewed at McCall for more than a dozen years. Louis felt that he needed to freshen things up, but he really didn't want to make a move. "Change and me are not really good. So I decided to bring on somebody who [could] get on with Greg." At this point, everybody at the table started to nervously laugh. "Somebody who was cantankerous. I needed Greg to train somebody."

That somebody became Edgar Newstadt, who was bartending at the time. "Cantankerous" doesn't really do Edgar justice. As the resident character of the brewery, if there is a loud happy hour conversation going on, you can usually find the jovial and friendly Newstadt at the middle of it. He also has been known to rep the brewery at beer festivals and events. If you have met somebody from McCall Brewing Company, chances are it was Edgar Newstadt—chances are also good that you came away feeling that this person loves McCall Brewing Company beer.

"I never even home-brewed!" exclaimed Edgar. "Nothing. So, I just started immediately into commercial brewing." Soon Edgar was coming up with recipes and had taken over the brewing operation. He had gone from bartender to head brewer in six short months. But that wasn't the whole story for the turnaround at McCall Brewing Company. That was only the beginning.

"We've spent a ton of money in the last year on equipment. A double-batch brite tank, a keg machine and lots of odds and ends. Stainless steel. It

The brew team at McCall Brewing Company: head brewer Edgar Newstadt and brewmaster Thom Tash.

McCall Brewing's unofficial mascot and head brewer Edgar Newstadt helps out behind the bar.

adds up," offered brewmaster Thom Tash about his new toys. The purpose of this expansion: bottling. In the entire list of things that they purchased, you will not find a bottler.

"I took the seventy to seventy-five grand that it would have cost on the bottling machine and spent like $90,000 on kegs!" barked Klinge when asked about the lack of a bottler. So, the path that every McCall bottle that can be purchased at bottle shops across Idaho takes starts with these three guys lining up and hand-bottling each and every beer they package. "It's an assembly line," laughed Edgar. "We can pump out fifty cases in three and a half hours."

The beers that McCall puts out now are far and away the best that have come out of the brewery. The Lemon-Ginger Hefeweizen, containing the refreshing nature of wheat with a snap of ginger and a citrusy finish, never fails to surprise at tastings. Devious Intent Imperial Stout is a bold, hoppy imperial stout that sits like tar in your glass, dark and murky as a puddle of Texas crude. It drinks smooth, with notes of chocolate, molasses and sweet smoke, inviting you to get more devious with each sip. Minimalist Bane and Hippie Hopped Pale Ale are two different sides of the pale ale coin. Bane is a biscuity English-style IPA, and Hippie, a delightfully hoppy West Coast–style pale ale, and both are crafted beautifully. McCall's most famous brew, Wobbily Man Scotch Ale, is so good that Idaho's resident Scot and beer connoisseur Natalie Steele, from Rudy's A Cook's Paradise in Twin Falls, calls it the single beer she could see selling nationally—she sells a case of it per week in her bottle shop.

"It was doing great, and we decided to take it to the next level and got Thom back," finished Klinge, with a look toward his brewmaster, Thom Tash. You might not have heard of Tash, but you have heard of the breweries that fill out his résumé. With stints at 10 Barrel Brewing, Barley Brown's and Kona Brewing, as well as two stints at McCall Brewing Company, Thom was working in Hawaii for Kona when Louis decided that he needed Tash back at McCall.

Thom had left Louis and Edgar to go to Kona, but not before he told the duo that he would gladly come back when they decided to expand the brewery. As soon as Thom left, Louis claimed that he and Edgar decided that they needed him right back.

"Edgar and I are like, 'Maybe we want to expand,'" started Louis, as Edgar nodded knowingly. "I flew to Hawaii to talk to Thom, then I flew Edgar and his wife over there to see if we had the same game plan." They didn't just bring Thom back to McCall; they brought back all the techniques that he had picked up along the way. It also meant that the small, formerly failed brewery in a town of about three thousand would be going through an expansion.

Thom doesn't just bring big brewery experience with him. He brings all the little techniques and tricks that only a seasoned brewer would have in his brewing tool kit. The first thing you notice when you drink the Lemon-Ginger Hefeweizen is that the ginger tastes like ginger and not the overly spiced nutmegy version often found in ginger beers. "We use real lemon zest and ginger," Edgar told me. "We chop it ourselves and peel it and zest it and put it in the boil. We're purists, really."

The easygoing Thom began, "I generally don't make too many rules that are hard-and-fast rules, but one of them is we're never going to use extract. Extract flavorings and aromas in this brewery—it just doesn't work for me." Louis chimed in that they are "a no-filter, no-extract" brewery. "We're pretty pure."

Anybody can chop up coconut, put it in the boil and call the beer a coconut porter, but not everybody makes a coconut porter like McCall. Thom brought the recipe from Kona, refined it for McCall Brewing and soon started filling lucky pub-goers' pint glasses and growlers with the delicious brew. The secret, Thom said, is how you manipulate the coconut, and it isn't how you think.

The coconut is chopped and put into the brite tank, instead of the fermenter or kettle, to "leach" out the creamy nuttiness and subtle sweetness of the coconut. "If you put the coconut on the hot side, you lose a lot of those flavors. If you put it into the fermenter, you're going to see a lot of aromas scrubbed away by carbonation," Thom informed the table. "The alcohol is in there to fight contamination, and it's the best way to get the aromatics out of the coconut. It takes a little bit more time, but it's the best way to get those aromatics out."

The result is Coconut Porter, a silky smooth, rich, English-style porter with just a bit of sweetness and creamy body imparted by the real coconut infused into the beer during the very last part of the brewing process. It's an unbelievably complex beer found at a small brewery in a tiny lake town.

The Brewing Scene in Sun Valley

If Idaho is the "playground for America," then Sun Valley is the part of the playground with the awesome slide and gold-plated jungle gym

Sawtooth Brewing's taproom, in Ketchum.

tucked behind a velvet rope. Sun Valley is a paradise for the rich and famous and was built exactly for that by two really rich and powerful guys: Union Pacific chairman W. Averell Harriman and Austrian nobleman Count Felix Schaffgotsch. They created the resort in 1936, according to *Forbes* magazine, to rival the great resorts of the European Alps. The two reasons they reportedly chose the valley beneath the Sawtooth Mountain Range was because it was close to the railroad and because it was hard to find. Ketchum and the Wood River Valley were the perfect places to build a place where the rich could go and never be found. Movie stars like Clark Gable, Gary Cooper and Ingrid Bergman became the first big stars to come out, spending their time and money in this remote area of Idaho. Current stars and moguls like Bill Gates, Demi Moore, Arnold Schwarzenegger, Robin Williams and Clint Eastwood have owned or still own property in Sun Valley.

Sun Valley's most famous resident, however, was not known for exploits on the screen but rather off it. Ernest Hemingway wrote much of his masterpiece *For Whom the Bell Tolls* at Sun Valley Lodge and died in his home there in 1961. There are spots along one of the many walking trails that show where Hemingway wrote and walked, as well as a monument to him on Ketchum's Main Street.

Hailey, Idaho (population 7,920), is home to the first brewpub you see on the way up to Sun Valley Resort: Sun Valley Brewing Company. In what is a microcosm of the area, Sun Valley Brewing Company is tucked away on Main Street next to some local grub spots and four- and five-star restaurants. It welcomes you with a large, ornate bar upon entering and tempts you with a dozen beers on tap. Pine Top Pale Ale, by far its most popular, is a citrusy West Coast–style pale that offers a bit of sweetness and nice overall flavor.

Going up the main road a bit, you come upon the town of Ketchum (population 3,873). Ketchum is the nerve center of Sun Valley, offering trendy, expensive wine bars and restaurants alongside blue-collar bars and eateries. Ketchum is a wonderful town to walk in, with shops, restaurants, coffee and bars all within blocks of the city center, which offers plenty of free parking for skiers just off the slope looking for a bite to eat or a pitcher to share. On the outskirts of this block radius stands Ketchum's first, and only, brewery and taproom: Sawtooth Brewery.

Founded in 2011 by brewer Paul Holle and business manager Kevin Jones, Sawtooth sought to bring fresh, handcrafted beers to Ketchum residents and tourists alike. The tap house features several Sawtooth beers, as well as some really nice local taps that often include premium craft beers from Sierra Nevada, Lagunitas, Epic Brewing and others from around the country, plus a cask option for "real ale" drinkers.

The brew house itself is a twenty-gallon system purchased from MoreBeer! Sawtooth outgrew this system almost immediately and has since contract-brewed with neighbor Sun Valley Brewing, as well as on the three-barrel system at Portneuf Valley Brewing in Pocatello.

The growth of Sawtooth has been impressive. Behind its signature beer, Freeheeler Rye IPA, Sawtooth tap handles can be found all over Sun Valley. Things have gotten so busy for Paul and the gang that in late 2013, Sawtooth began hand-bottling three beers to sell in local stores. So, bottle shoppers in Ketchum and Hailey can pick up Freeheeler Rye IPA, Sheepherder Saison and a rotating seasonal brew in twenty-two-ounce bottles.

The residents and visitors of Ketchum have a lot to look forward to from Sawtooth. With expansion plans that include a production brewery, barrel aging, canning and a casual restaurant, the playground for America's rich will soon be a playground for fans of delicious, locally crafted beer.

IDAHO PUB CRAWL

The neighborhood brewpub—a place where you can sit down, have a freshly made beer and chat with friends, old and new. The stainless steel or copper brew kettles normally sit somewhere inside the pub where you can watch your favorite beverages grow from sacks of malt to a beer in your hand. Brewpubs are one of those things that have transcended cultures, and oceans, to become not just a staple in your town but also a staple of humanity just about everywhere on the planet.

Before Prohibition, Idaho was littered with brewpubs (for a complete list, see the appendix). During the gold and silver rush days of the late 1800s and early 1900s, there were pubs in just about every mining town and major population center in Idaho.

Chain pubs have become the American bastardization of brewpubs, with a few exceptions. The Ram in Boise makes delicious beers year round, and many of the head brewers in the Gem State learned their craft from the brewers there. Even today, when you want a quality growler on a Sunday in Boise, The Ram is your best bet to be open and pouring its delicious IPAs, ambers and red ales into your sixty-four-ounce containers. Many chain pubs have one operational brewery in a city and get all their beer from that one brewery instead of brewing it themselves. Put a *Mc* on the front of any of these places, and people would stop going. However, the shiny stainless tanks stay shiny, people order the pizza and the world continues to spin.

So, what are we left with? After that rush of openings and closures, Idaho has a fairly impressive array of independently owned and operated brewpubs around the state. Places like Bertrum's Salmon Valley Brewery in Salmon and MJ Barleyhoppers in Lewiston are serving up fresh beers to their regulars and cooking up some fantastic food. Wallace Brewing Company offers its beers in twelve- and twenty-two-ounce bottles for thirsty folks in the Panhandle to take home and drink. McCall Brewing Company has changed owners a few times but now makes outstanding beer and food alongside new neighbor Salmon River Brewery, which has just moved, taking its backyard vibe to the shores of Payette Lake close by. Sockeye Brewing's second iteration was, and still is, a brewpub on Cole and Ustick in Boise. The Ram opened back up in 1995 and has become a breeding ground for the state's best brewers.

There is a story to Idaho's brewpub scene, and the logical way to tell it is to start at the beginning, with Boise's own TableRock Brewpub.

TableRock Brewpub

TableRock Brewpub lies in the heart of Boise, just across the river from Boise State University in downtown Boise. This establishment has been part of the Idaho brew scene since 1991.

"Historically, this brewery was the original Boise Brewery. So, the guy who started [TableRock] had a pretty good idea," said Chris Nelson, current owner of the city's oldest brewpub. "He got a pretty decent location as far as the city is concerned."

Soon after TableRock opened, the owners decided that it was time to start literally bottling up that success. So they opened a big bottling plant a few miles away in Meridian, and the rest is history. Not entirely a happy history, though. The owners, for whatever reason, could not make distribution work. Chris Nelson believes that it was a conspiracy to shut the little guy out of the market, but many others believe that it just wasn't the right time to bottle up brewpub beer.

"So, TableRock back in the mid- to late '90s had a bottling program; they were bottling six-packs," Brewforia owner Rick Boyd said. "And they failed at it miserably. Partly because of the quality of the beer and partly because the market wasn't ready for craft beer."

But TableRock didn't close. Nelson, a real estate mogul of sorts in downtown Boise, as well as somebody who had home-brewed in the '80s and was a patron of TableRock, rescued the brewpub in 2008. "I liked the place," said Nelson. "So, I figured it was better to pick up the pieces to keep it going then let it whither and die."

The new ownership didn't bring many changes to the failing brewpub until a year ago, when Nelson decided that he had had enough of the old and wanted to see his newly acquired pub evolve. "The beers had not changed in eighteen to twenty years. And I personally was getting tired of the beer. I think everybody was getting just a little bit weary. It was November of last year. I made the executive decision that we're going to throw out the whole old, and we're going to start from scratch and just start again."

This decision proved to be less of a shot in the arm for TableRock and more of a leap of faith. The head brewer at the time, Tim Spanbauer, "jumped right on board," according to Nelson, and they began to rewrite and break down all of TableRock's recipes. Soon after, Spanbauer got an offer from Sockeye's owners to brew for them and left. In came Kerry Caldwell, formerly of Belmont Brewpub in Long Beach, California, and she

A beautiful wooden inlaid logo of Boise's oldest brewpub, TableRock.

brought a wealth of knowledge on brewing and barrel aging. She left within the year to take over as head brewer at the new Edge Brewery in Boise.

Nelson finally found the brewer he wanted in the form of Derek Anderson, who had worked his way up the ladder at The Ram and was ready to be a head brewer. Nelson then brought in his old friend Justin Cole to act as assistant brewer, and all of a sudden, he had the right team to move forward. "We kind of cobbled together a brew program," said Nelson, "and have really been hitting the ground running."

Not just any brew program either; TableRock has been on the forefront of experimental beers and meads in the Boise area. "We'd like to be somewhat dynamic from the standpoint that you come in and you're intrigued to try something that you may not normally want to try," head brewer Derek Anderson told me. "You come in here, and you're going to see [that] probably at least half of our list will be new things; they're going to be experimental, they're going to be barreled [and] they're going to be sour."

True to his word, Derek sat me down and had me try a few of his tap offerings, which included a seldom seen kristallweizen and a sage-infused mead. The mead was fantastic, with the perfect amount of herbs to peppery mead flavor and a lightness you don't normally get from an 11 percent beverage. He also turned me on to a barrel-aged sour rye-saison that was a Pro-Am contest winner; it was wonderfully sour with just a little rye bite.

TableRock has focused on staying local as well. With beer and mead on tap, you can expect to find a lot of fresh, local ingredients in both beverages. "We get all of our base malt and our silo malt right from Pocatello," Derek Anderson said about locally sourced ingredients. "We did a pomegranate mead, and one of our customers brought us a ton of pomegranates. We source our honey here in Idaho as well. The honey all comes out of Salmon, Idaho. Hops are from over on Alpha Hop Sales; we source them from Wilder…Anytime you can buy local and it's quality, it makes it easier to continue to buy that way as long as the product is good."

TableRock's new approach has garnered attention outside the walls as well. Rick Boyd, of Brewforia, is particularly excited about one of Boise's oldest breweries making its way back. "They were on the verge of collapse. Thankfully, they've managed to come back, and Derek, the new brewer, is doing an amazing job. He's making some fantastic beers."

Anderson, you can tell, has long thought about what his first shot as a head brewer would be like and he is focused on making the most of this opportunity. "We spend a lot of energy trying to make things that are good, as opposed to making things that are typical."

Portneuf Valley Brewing

Penny Pink is the kind of person who starts downhill skiing in November and is trying out double black diamond runs by March. She's the type of person who decides to build brewing equipment by driving her diesel Suburban from Pocatello to a salvage yard in Portland and loading every ounce of stainless steel bladders and tanks in and on top of said Suburban, driving home, teaching herself to do stainless steel finishing and then building her

The front of Portneuf Valley Brewing in Pocatello's historic Warehouse District.

own brewing system from that metal. She's the type of person who doesn't decide to be the first female head brewer in the state; she just does it. And she doesn't really give a damn about it.

"I've worked in male-dominated fields my entire career," Penny Pink said. "I'm a scientist. I was framing houses and working in gas stations as a teenager. I just don't let being a gal be a problem. If there's something I want to do, I just do it!"

Portneuf Valley Brewing was born from just that attitude—and only $5,000. Started eighteen years ago as the brewery for a now defunct local sports bar, Penny Pink turned her self-described "Franken-brew" system into a full-fledged brewpub in 2006. That was after "boot-strapping" (her words) her way from handling taps at a sports bar to buying and renovating her own building enough to start pouring beer and then building and opening a fully operational kitchen.

> *Penny Pink came to Idaho to be a microbiologist and stumbled onto brewing when her husband accidentally blew up a batch on his power tools. "I won't repeat exactly what he said, but it was something along the lines of, 'Woman, you're the one with degrees in biology and chemistry, you brew the beer.'" She began to home-brew, and there were soon carboys all over her house.*

The building she bought in 1999 was basically a run-down building in an abandoned warehouse district that lies between the freeway and downtown Pocatello. True to form, Penny didn't really care that the dilapidated building was previously used as a haunted house ("There was a skeleton hanging in my elevator"), that the floors had to be stripped down to the floor joist, that the roof leaked or that her oldest son called it "a gutted shit hole" when she bought it. She didn't care because she's Penny Pink and because, much like that pile of scrap metal, she saw something special in that building.

"This building used to be the bottling plant for East Idaho Brewing Company in the post-Prohibition years up until the mid-'50s," Penny told me while sitting in the newly remodeled top floor of her now completely renovated (and beautiful) nine-thousand-square-foot brewpub. "Then it was an auto parts warehouse, and they had asphalted over the old brewery floors and filled in the copper drain trench. It was in really rough shape. These hardwood floors were literally black." In other words, it was quite the fixer-upper.

"My two sons and I, who were in junior high/high school age at that point; some of Pocatello's finest spiked and pierced young men; and a few girls thrown in there for inspiration basically in their infinite free time started gutting the building out. So we spent three years gutting the building out."

They finished up just in time. Dudley's Sports Bar, where Penny was pouring her delicious beers, was about to close. Penny's brewery at Dudley's was inside an old post office, where the vault was her grain room. When Dudley's closed in 2002, she had a month to get out and was faced with a tough decision. Should she get her dilapidated building up to code, move in and start up a brewpub or go back to an environmental science career that paid better but forced her away from her growing boys?

Penny chose both. She gutted and renovated enough of her building to carve out an area to brew and pour beers, trained somebody to brew her beers and then went back to work at Idaho National Lab, seventy-five miles away in the desert, where she managed people to take care of hazardous waste. As soon as the taproom proved profitable, she went to the bank, took out a loan, built the kitchen and hasn't looked back.

The "Franken-brew" system Penny built from scrap metal served her well for thirteen years. It was built from old soda-making tanks and originally set up to do two barrels at a time. She quickly figured out that two barrels wouldn't cut it and reconfigured the tanks to brew three barrels. It was a three-vessel system with a hot liquor tank, a mash and lauter tun and a boiling kettle. For fermenting, she bought a bunch of fifty-five-gallon sealed drums, and for brite tanks, she bought used Golden Gate kegs. The Golden Gate kegs were perfect for brite tanks because they each had a lager arm that extended into the tank and pulled beer slightly off the bottom, thus leaving no sediment. "As long as I didn't move the kegs, I would have nice, clean, bright beer!" She was able to sell the "Franken-Brew" system after buying a brand-new professional three-barrel system in 2010.

She didn't just renovate that building; she lifted up an entire neighborhood. The warehouse district, once abandoned but for a troupe of thrill-seeking gymnasts, is now a vibrant part of the city. "When I bought this building, there was nothing going on in this district," said Pink. "I've seen a lot of case studies where—Denver's a great example—where people will come into an old historic warehouse district, put in a brewpub and that becomes a catalyst for redevelopment for that district."

Portneuf Valley Brewing is more than just a brewpub to Pocatello; it's a community center. Take a look at Portneuf's Facebook page, and you will notice events, concerts and a whole lot of other things you wouldn't necessarily think would happen at a brewpub. Pink added that they host things "like science seminars and other cultural events. How many times can you go to a science seminar and enjoy a beer?"

You can't discuss Portneuf Valley Brewing and not talk about the incredible artwork that adorns the tap handles, T-shirts and posters all around inside. The exceptional artwork on such brands as Krystal Weizen, Ligertown Lager and Midnight Satin Cream Stout speak to the fun and creative nature that Penny has tried to infuse into her brewpub. The artwork holds a special place in her heart, as her eldest son did most of the graphics.

Portneuf Valley Brewing doesn't just have beautiful artwork and a building full of character; it also has really good beer. With most of the tap list coming in at under 5 percent alcohol by volume, Penny maximizes the flavor profiles of her beers without succumbing to the pressures of creating high-octane brews. "What I've tried to do is make some flavorful beers; people can come in, and they can responsibly have a couple of beers and be able to get home without being stupid about it."

The beers are very flavorful. Midnight Satin, one of the only of its kind produced in Idaho, is a wonderful milk stout, with a creamy mouth feel and notes of dark chocolate. Penny's Extra Pale is a classic pale ale, refreshing and bright, with flavors of sweet malt and a bit of citrus hops to balance it out. Ligertown Lager is a wonderful light lager, with crisp, grassy hops on

Left: You always hook something good at Sockeye Brewpub in Boise.

Below: McCall Brewing Company.

Left: Selkirk Abbey's Infidel IPA bottle.

Below: The classic sign hanging up above Bier:Thirty, Boise's east end beer restaurant in Bown Crossing.

Opposite, top: Copper tap handles of Bogus Brewing. *Courtesy Bogus Brewing.*

Opposite, bottom: Boise's most popular IPA, Sockeye Dagger Falls IPA.

Left: Part of Kris Price's "artistic" brewery, a copper-headed kettle bought from Anheuser-Busch.

Below: Beautiful metal-worked tap handles on display in Crooked Fence's taproom.

A beautiful handmade dragon tap handle along with Kilted Dragon's other tap handles at its taproom on Chinden Street in Garden City. Kilted's three-barrel brew house can be seen in the background.

The tap handles at Grand Teton's taproom in Victor, Idaho.

Victor, Idaho, home to Grand Teton and Wildlife breweries.

Two-row barley roasting in the kiln room at Great Western Malting in Pocatello.

A huge mound of hops waiting to be bailed and sold at Gooding Farms in Parma.

Bravo hops on the vine at Gooding Farms in Parma.

Above: TableRock brewpub head brewer Derek Anderson takes a long look at his handiwork.

Left: Penny Pink, head brewer, founder and owner of Portneuf Valley Brewing in Pocatello.

Left: Amazing artwork that adorns the tap handles, T-shirts and posters inside Portneuf Valley Brewing in Pocatello.

Below: Payette Brewing Company's brand-new canning line.

Matt Ganz and Matt Hurlbutt standing in front of the new Salmon River Brewpub on the banks of Payette Lake in McCall.

One of Idaho's finest brews, Sweetgrass American Pale Ale, being bottled up at Grand Teton Brewing.

Picked hops and harvested fields at Obendorf Hop Inc. in Parma.

Rick Boyd, owner of Brewforia Beer Markets and Grind Modern Burger, started the bottle shop because he wanted to buy better beer.

Above: 10 Barrel Brewing's little secret stash of Pub Beer, an American light lager brewed in Bend and sold exclusively at 10 Barrel Brewpubs.

Left: The tap handle for 10 Barrel Brewing's collaboration with Stone Brewing and Blue Jacket, Suede Imperial Porter, at 10 Barrel Brewpub in Boise.

Opposite, top: Dave Krick, owner of Bittercreek Alehouse and Red Feather Restaurant, stands inside his newly renovated dining space.

Opposite, bottom: Bogus Brewing has plenty of growlers in 2014, but will its beer be filling them in 2015? Only time will tell.

Above: Sweetgrass APA bottles coming out of Grand Teton's newly upgraded bottling system, which can bottle twelve-ounce bottles or be converted (in only three hours) to bottle twenty-two-ounce bombers.

Right: Grand Teton Brewing, Idaho's most prolific brewery, started life as Otto Brothers' Brewing across the border in Wyoming.

Crooked Fence's "Am-Brew-Lance" sits outside its Garden City brewery ready for any "beer-mergency!"

Payette head brewer Ian Fuller stands in front of the newly installed canning line. Before installing its own line, Payette utilized a "mobile canning" service to can its delicious beers.

Hops ain't no joke over at Laughing Dog Brewing, where owner and Head Brewer Fred Colby brews eight IPAs throughout the year.

Above, left: A coaster from the former Coeur d'Alene Brewing Company, which was forced to move out of its downtown building before finally closing for good in 2010.

Above, right: Muggers was the hot spot in Twin Falls for much of the '90s before closing in 2006.

Beautiful artwork designed by Penny Pink's son adorns the handles at Portneuf Valley Brewing.

the finish. Krystal Weizen is an American wheat that finishes smooth. Gorg IPA has notes of pine and citrus, with a strong malt backbone typical of an English-style IPA. Penny's beers are flavorful and balanced.

She isn't going to stop anytime soon, either. Portneuf Valley Brewing will continue to be a fixture in Pocatello. "Everything's paid for. The building's paid for. Everything in it is paid for. I think that's a success."

Highlands Hollow Brewhouse

Highlands Hollow Brewhouse opened up in Bogus Basin, just north of Boise, in May 1992 under the name Harrison Hollow Brewhouse. Original brewer Jim Fishwild had a very forward-thinking approach back then for his brewery: to make hoppy beers. "Our brewery was sort of on the cutting edge of the hop revolution," said current head brewer and twenty-year employee Chris Compton about the beginnings of Boise's second-oldest brewpub.

Those original hoppy ales were, and largely still are, English-based beers. "They were doing what in the mid-'90s was popular: making their English-style ales," said Bittercreek Alehouse owner Dave Krick. Those bitter, English ales are largely still available from the brewery, although the end almost came for Highlands Hollow.

The brewpub was forced to close when the original owners went into Chapter 11 bankruptcy. The reorganization meant new ownership in the form of Rod Davidson. Davidson, like TableRock's new owner, owned the property that Harrison Hollow was on and wanted to keep the brewpub open. "The family that owned the property kind of empowered the people who had run it for years," Krick said of the ownership change. "They've done a really nice job with it, considering their struggles."

Like Krick said, the new ownership kept many of the same employees and provided leadership that has kept the popular post-ski pub in business for the past dozen years. "Today, we employ many people who have worked here for over ten years," said head brewer Chris Compton. "In fact, more than half the staff goes back even farther."

The beers have stayed decidedly English and refreshingly bitter after more than twenty years of brewing in Bogus Basin. "We brew many of the same beers that we brewed here twenty years ago, combined with more contemporary styles," said Compton. Highlands Hollow has continued to distribute around Boise, with about twenty accounts that receive kegs from one of Boise's oldest brewpubs.

Wildlife Brewing

What's better than pizza and beer? Hot, cheesy slices of pizza with cold, refreshing, sweet beer has been a go-to meal since beer made its way from Mesopotamia to Italy. It's always a perfect pairing, and that is why Ric Harmon decided to change Wildlife from a takeout pizza stop in Victor to a full-on pizza brewpub. It only meant literally turning his home into his business.

What started out as a pizza takeout place in his garage soon meant that Wildlife owner Ric had to kick tenant Ric out of the house and go through some major renovations. He converted his house and backyard into what is now the bar and restaurant portion of his pub and further expanded his kitchen, building an area for his ten-barrel brew house and finding spots for fermenters and a grain room.

That's not all. Ric went out and found a used barley silo that he turned into space for more fermenters and a brite tank and is now able to self-distribute his brews as far south as Pocatello. "We are a lifestyle brewery. We

Wildlife Brewpub and Pizzeria in Victor. You can see the silo that houses extra tanks.

promote living the wild life and the natural wildlife we get to share our home with," Ric said about his brewery's focus.

Walking around the pub, Ric casually pointed to things like the bathroom doors, where his couch used to be, or the ornate, custom-made bar with a hand-made overhanging shelf where his "mug club" patrons keep their glassware that used to be his back porch. You notice the sort of puzzle-like way he's managed to fit in all his various brewing tanks and cooking equipment together in the spot where he used to park his car and wonder how the beers will eventually taste once they wind their way through this crazy amalgamation of pipes and pizza dough into the serving tanks and eventually into your glass.

Terrific is how they taste. A Harvest Ale Ric made in his ten-barrel brew house, which he bought used from a brewery in Florida, with 100 percent Mosaic hops and Crisp Maris Otter malt is simply fantastic and something that I would want served in my neighborhood bar. The hops' flavors of tropical fruit, grapefruit flesh and just a bit of pine come through wonderfully with the caramel sweetness of the malt, creating a fantastic harvest ale. A second brew, Buckwild Double Blonde Ale, is an altogether different beer but just as amazing. Tasting almost like a cream ale with a kick—at just over 6 percent alcohol by volume and dry-hopped with spicy Amarillo hops—this blonde doesn't play around.

This isn't just a brewpub for locals. With only about two thousand full-time residents and two breweries, Victor, Idaho, enjoys the spoils of being the gateway to Yellowstone Park in the summer and right around the corner from Jackson, Wyoming, in the winter. Ric said that tourists make up just about half of his business, and "they are shocked that our little town has two great breweries."

It's no puzzle why Wildlife Brewing has been in business for just over a decade, proving that even in the smallest of towns, there's always room for pizza and beer.

10 Barrel Brewing Brewpub

When 10 Barrel Brewing opened up in the historic Sherm Building on the corner of Bannock and Ninth Street in downtown Boise, even Boise beer scene fixture Bittercreek Alehouse felt the pain of having a legitimate brewpub, from an established brewery, land just a few blocks from its steps. Dave Krick, owner of Bittercreek Alehouse, summed it up best: "They kicked our ass all summer. 10 Barrel is awesome. Shawn is making some great beer. We were down 15 percent all summer; it hurt."

That Shawn he's referring to is Shawn Kelso, head brewer at 10 Barrel Brewing Boise and about as far from an ass-kicker as you could get. Personable and always pleasant, Shawn had to rely on patience before finally ascending to his current post in downtown Boise.

"I was hired to come here," said Shawn. "I was working in a pub in Baker City [Oregon], Barley Browns, for eleven years, and they called me up and made me an offer and I accepted. But it was about a year, actually fifty weeks and thirty-seven thousand miles, that I drove back and forth [from Bend to Boise]." He continued, "It took a little while. We were going to open actually two years ago last June, and that's when I first committed, and it was going to be a hurry-up thing."

The pub finally opened on April 22, 2013, to rave reviews and thirsty customers. The brew part of the 10 Barrel Brewing pub is evident as soon as you walk in and spot the huge, classically shaped bar with an equally

10 Barrel Brewing on Ninth and Bannock in Downtown Boise.

Shawn Kelso, head brewer at 10 Barrel Brewing Boise, standing in his brand-new ten-barrel brew house.

impressive chalk tap list hanging on the exposed brick wall. To the immediate left are giant shiny stainless steel tanks, separated from diners by only a railing—no glass! On the bar are twenty or so classic taproom handles, with a few special ones sticking up out of the bar. On this day, it was recent 10 Barrel/Stone/Blue Jacket Collaboration Suede Imperial Porter that had just come on tap.

> *10 Barrel Brewing gutted out the near century-old Sherm Building and left it looking, well, gutted. Exposed brick walls go up about two and a half stories to exposed beam ceilings from which hang giant industrial lights and exhaust fans. The entrance gives you two options: bar or restaurant. The restaurant area, family-friendly of course, stretches down the west side of the building, giving diners an excellent look out into downtown Boise. What would a "10 Barrel" brewpub be without barrels? The barrel aging room, with a climate-controlled humidor in the middle of the restaurant, holds Shawn's delicious barrel-aged creations, as well as oak-cured meats that are served in the restaurant.*

Looking at the tap list, you see the excellent year-round 10 Barrel beers that include Apocalypse IPA, O.G. Wheat and Sinistor Black Ale. You wouldn't normally think that a brewpub that comes in from out of state would be so into using ingredients from the state of Idaho, but 10 Barrel Brewing doesn't stop at the locally sourced lamb. One of Shawn's passions is brewing beers made with fruits and vegetables sourced from local farms.

During the fall, when it was time to produce a pumpkin beer, Shawn spoke with his friends at Peaceful Belly, just outside Boise, and contracted heirloom Cinderella and Lux pumpkins to use in his brew. The taste is fantastic, with just a little spice to set the beer off; you truly get a beautiful toasted pumpkin flavor from his pumpkin ale.

It doesn't stop there. When Shawn wanted to do a jalapeño beer, he once again contacted the people at Peaceful Belly. "Hotland, gary and wax, pimento…what else," said an excited Shawn about his newest creation. "I put one in called Inferno and then a sweet cayenne. It turned out really good. It's all organic."

Peaceful Pepper Ale, in which Shawn dumped fifteen pounds of locally sourced peppers, was fantastic. Built into a cream ale, the spicy jalapeño kick is just enough to get your attention but not enough to leave you reaching for a glass of water to cool down. "It's really good with pizza," crooned Kelso, as the jalapeño beer goes down.

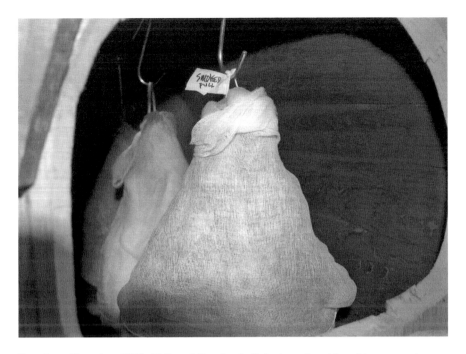

Barrel-aged beer is so 2012; 10 Barrel Brewing in Boise has a humidor with preserved meat aging next to beers in oak barrels.

"Well worth the wait" is how most Boise residents would describe the arrival of 10 Barrel Brewing's downtown pub. With delicious locally sourced food and mouthwatering specialty beers, 10 Barrel has quickly become a fixture of Boise's beer scene.

Idaho Falls' Pair of Pubs

The Mountain Brewers Beer Festival, held annually in Idaho Falls by the North American Brewers Association, is the place to be if you are either in the beer scene or want to be a part of the beer scene in the Mountain West. This includes Idaho, Oregon, Washington, Wyoming, Montana, western Colorado and Utah.

"It's the best beer fest in Utah," said Andy Shaw, Idaho Falls' Snow Eagle Brewing & Grill's head brewer, Cargill Malting maintenance manager and Mountain Brewer Fest judge. The newly minted Snow Eagle, which moved into the building formerly occupied by failed brewpub Brownstone Brewing in

Idaho Brewing Company in Idaho Falls.

April 2012, has a very important role in the Mountain Brewer Festival—after-party headquarters for the brewers attending the festival—mostly because of its walking distance from the former Red Lion Hotel (now called Hotel on the Falls) in downtown Idaho Falls.

"There's nothing like having 150 of your close peers that are all brewers show up to that hotel right there and every one of them end up right here in your place," Shaw said about hosting fellow brewers. "It was kind of tough my first year because my first eight batches were experimental batches. Its kind of a weight on your shoulders to have 150 to 200 freaking brewer friends of yours drinking your beer."

The festival, which hosts more than six thousand thirsty revelers and takes over the whole town, is probably the second-most-important competition for mountain brewers outside the Great American Beer Festival. The awards are highly sought after by breweries in each of the states around Idaho and hang proudly on the walls beside, not under, GABF medals.

Andy Shaw made his way to Idaho Falls by way of Germany, Utah and Los Angeles. "I was born and raised in LA. Moved to Heber [Utah] when I was twelve. Joined the army to get the fuck out of there," Shaw said about how he got to Germany. That country turned out to be a blessing for the young enlisted man. The father of his first girlfriend overseas owned a brewery, and that's where Andy learned to love really good beer. He took that love of beer back to the States, where he soon got a job at the old Brownstone Brewpub in Idaho Falls.

Andy had guest-brewed at eleven breweries, including The Ram in Boise, the old Trail Creek in Twin Falls, Bitterroot Brewing in Montana, Wolf Pack in West Yellowstone and Utah Brewer's Cooperative and Red Rock Brewing Company in Salt Lake City. This adventurous attitude has led Shaw to experiment in his own brewery, bringing home an award for an experimental winter warmer mixed with Sauvignon Blanc grape juice and Nelson Sauvin hops.

He first started commercially brewing at Brownstone after being an avid home-brewer. In fact, he's still an avid home-brewer, with a refrigerator filled with his own meads and heavily hopped IPAs. "I have a keg of home-brew, a 10 percent double black IPA that's got a pound of Simcoe in it. I took a keg of my IPA and put a pound of Citra in it." Just to put Shaw's love of hops in perspective, a heavily hopped five-gallon batch of beer will normally have up to about five or six ounces of hops in it.

Snow Eagle Brewing & Grill is unique in that it has both pub food and a separate sushi restaurant. This is something that Andy has embraced as a new challenge to the beer pairings he loves to do. "We're getting ready to do a sushi and beer pairing. The IPA is bold enough to handle something hot. What I'm going to do is a spicy Sriracha tuna roll for the IPA."

The head brewing gig is only a part-time one for Shaw, his "other" job being the maintenance manager at Cargill's malting plant in Idaho Falls. The maintenance manager, the second-most important job in the plant, is in charge of making sure everything in the plant keeps working. That allows him some perks that other head brewers probably don't get. "I get all my malt through Cargill. I'm the only person in Cargill history to get bulk malt at an employee discount, ever."

Idaho Brewing Company takes a more conservative approach, and it isn't really a pub but rather more of a taproom. "I don't know that we have necessarily a focus where we want to be outside the box," said Idaho Brewing Company head brewer Matt Spann about his brewery's more traditional approach to beer. "We do specialize in more traditional type beers."

It's not for nothing either, as Idaho Brewing Company has carved out a clientele and fan base around eastern and southern Idaho by crafting beers that aren't extreme but rather are extremely flavorful. Behind the flagship Black Lager, a three-time gold medal winner, Idaho Brewing Company has put its mark on Idaho's brewing community by going the way of the old turtle: slow and steady.

Idaho Brewing Company's Black Lager is an excellent judge of the brewery because of the simple flavors that are done perfectly in a style that can easily be screwed up. The beer pours black and thin, like coffee, with roasted malt and faint hop aromas that play subtly on the nose. Flavors of coffee, chocolate and sweet, roasted malts give way to light hop bitterness and a clean finish from the Bavarian lager yeast. An excellent, simple beer full of character and flavor.

Matt came aboard about a year and a half after Leon "Wolf" Wolfram opened the brewery in 2009. Matt, much like Leon, came from an environmental science background, doing assessments for new wind farms, oil fields and pipelines for a consulting company. He decided that he was tired of living in a pickup truck half the time and in a crummy hotel room in North Dakota the other half, so he made a change. "Why not try something that you're really passionate about? And at that time, it was brewing," Matt said about his life-changing decision. "Thought I might try that."

Matt arrived at Idaho Brewing Company and quickly rose up the chain, becoming head brewer after about six months on the job. "I just kind of worked into the position where we both felt comfortable." That move turned out to be an excellent one for Wolf and Idaho Brewing Company. It freed Wolf up to focus more on the business and got Matt going on building more recipes for Idaho Brewing Company's loyal customers—beers like the pre-Prohibition lager being sipped on during the interview.

"We put some research into it and decided to use an old variety cluster [hop], which has fallen out of fashion," explained Matt about the lager, which is a nice and traditional though darkly tinted, malty lager that goes down easy and tastes great. Matt used about a couple pounds of Black Prince malt, a de-husked, de-bittered black roasted malt that gives it a little bit of color.

Matt has also had tremendous success with his other beers. Two of his first beers ended up doing very well for Idaho Brewing Company. His ESB won a silver medal at the Mountain Brewers Festival, and his

Matt Spann, head brewer at Idaho Brewing Company, standing next to one of his pristine tanks.

Oktoberfest Marzen also took home a silver medal at Mountain Brewers and was quite popular in the pub. "I've had judges come up to us and say it's the best Oktoberfest they've ever had. People drink us out of it. First batch lasted three weeks."

That doesn't mean he rushed to brew and package the next batch. "Product quality is our number-one thing. We haven't sacrificed anything for volume."

PART III

GEM STATE BREWING
MAKING ITS OWN HISTORY

THE NORTHERN BREWING FRONT

According to most brewers in southern Idaho, there are two "big dogs" in Idaho's Panhandle that are brewing some seriously tasty beers: Laughing Dog and Selkirk Abbey.

Laughing Dog brews eight IPAs throughout the year, taking head brewer Fred Colby's love of lupulin to extremes most brewers won't attempt. Selkirk Abbey's head brewer, Jeff Whitman, decided to take his brewery in another direction, filling his catalogue full of delicious Belgian-style brews.

Another way these breweries have separated themselves from other Idaho brewers is that in order for Selkirk Abbey to open, Colby had to fight to get a law changed to allow him to have a vested interest in two breweries. His successful lobby to change the law made it so that Jeff Whitman could open Selkirk Abbey and put his delicious beers into the market.

These two breweries—along with Wallace Brewing, Trickster Brewing and Moscow Brewing Company—serve the northern Idaho Panhandle with fresh-made brews, as well as fantastic places to drink them.

Bottles and cans of beautiful Idaho beers on display at Brewforia in Eagle.

Laughing Dog Brewing

Fred Colby, co-owner, co-founder and head brewer of Laughing Dog Brewing Company, started the Ponderay brewery with a fondness for IPA and a desire to stay near Sandpoint, Idaho. So, in 2005, he opened up shop and started brewing his award-winning beers.

Colby has slowly built up his portfolio of beers since that time, picking up awards for a dozen of his beers. Fred started his new career with a fifteen-barrel brew house that has morphed into an eighteen-barrel version after a "drastic" modification. Laughing Dog did about two hundred barrels in its first year and then moved into a larger facility in 2010. Fred's small brewery has slowly grown into a fairly large brew house sporting a dozen thirty- and four sixty-barrel fermenters capable of doing fifteen thousand barrels of beer a year.

This slow and steady growth has been built on the backs of strong, consistent beers. "I love Fred at Laughing Dog," said Brewforia owner Rick

Boyd. "Fred has really played it safe. The beers that he produces are beers he knows are going to be commercially successful out of the gate."

In this age of hoppy, bitter beers owning the market, Laughing Dog has done something that some would call crazy: produce a bunch of IPAs. Colby produces eight IPAs over the year, including seven that have brought medals back to Ponderay. "Every brewery has got to have some kind of a signature and ours is the IPAs and the 'big' beers," Colby told the *Bonner County Daily Bee* back in 2010, when the brewery expanded to its new facility.

Colby's IPAs are exemplary. Alpha Dog Imperial IPA is one of the finest IPAs made in Idaho; with assertive and bold hop flavors of citrus and the sticky, resinous mouth feel of a big, imperial IPA, this is truly the top dog of IPAs in Idaho. Rocketdog Rye IPA, a citrusy West Coast IPA with a rye bite, is a wonderful mix of bitter hops and bready rye malt, giving Idaho beer lovers something that isn't really offered by the other state breweries. Laughing Dog IPA, available in cans and bottles, is a great example of what Fred likes about these beers, as it offers grapefruit zest and orange flesh flavors with mild malt cracker crunch that refreshes.

Laughing Dog isn't just doing it with bright West Coast IPAs either; perhaps its most sought-after beers are its line of dark beers. Beers like Anubis Coffee Porter and the Dogfather Barrel Aged Stout are just rumors to many people in Idaho because they are so hard to find on the open market.

"I think the Dogfather is a really fun beer," said Bittercreek Alehouse owner Dave Krick. "[Fred] was probably one of the first to really push quality on that side of the equation."

> *Laughing Dog's award-winning Huckleberry Cream Ale is a summer tradition for Idaho craft beer drinkers. With just enough fruit to tantalize the taste buds and not overwhelm the malty cream ale backbone, this fruit beer is just as good after a long day on the farm as it is with a lamb dinner. Laughing Dog uses real huckleberries at the end of the boil to maximize the unique flavor and aroma of Idaho's state fruit.*

Laughing Dog isn't just changing the game because of the beers it produces, but also because of how Fred and company have chosen to distribute those beers. Unlike any other brewery in Idaho, Laughing Dog distributes nationally with Total Wine & More, a Costco-sized liquor warehouse with 101 stores in fifteen states from coast to coast. This deal opens up huge beer markets for Laughing Dog like California, Texas, North Carolina, Florida, New Jersey and Virginia. "It's a nice arrangement," said Colby.

"Laughing Dog's IPA medaled at the GABF and is just one of their many beers that already sells nationally," added Selkirk Abbey co-owner and business partner Jeff Whitman about the Total Wine deal.

Exclusivity isn't necessarily a bad thing, but it certainly makes one's mouth water, especially in the case of these delicious dark brews. Perhaps one day, like the sweet success Fred Colby has spent the last ten years waiting for, we will be treated to Laughing Dog's delicious beers across the state, like those lucky dogs who shop at Total Wine & More.

Belgium on the Post Falls: Selkirk Abbey

Post Falls used to be the small town between Spokane, Washington, and Coeur d'Alene where one could do his or her outlet mall shopping, park a boat at Templin's for easy access to Lake Coeur d'Alene or take the family bowling at River City Lanes. As somebody whose first job was in Post Falls (at the now closed Jack in the Box near the Outlets), it was surprising to me when a brewery opened up on Seltice Way.

It was a shock that the brewery crafted only Belgian-style beers. But the taste of the brews from Selkirk Abbey has blown away everybody in Idaho. "Selkirk Abbey," responded Rick Boyd when asked which Idaho brewery could break out on the national stage, "because they're producing extremely high-quality, innovative and unique beers that are thoughtfully packaged and well presented."

Rob Mullin, brewmaster at Grand Teton Brewing, said that the beers coming out of Selkirk Abbey are "fun, interesting, different and high quality. Those are the kind of beers that have the most potential to capture the imagination of today's craft drinker."

"They're making really fun and different things that are outside the norm of what you find in the Boise market," raved Chris Oates, owner of Bier:Thirty.

"Selkirk has the innovation and the uniqueness and the top-shelf approach that we need," finished Boyd about the up-and-coming abbey that has opened on the shores of the Post Falls River.

"There are a number of reasons why Selkirk Abbey is a Belgian-centric brewery," started Jeff Whitman, co-founder, co-owner and head brewer of Selkirk Abbey. "The most important reason is that I absolutely love Belgian beer. Belgian beer is always in season and is where I'll go first and second and generally last."

That love for all things Belgian shines through in Whitman's beers. Infidel Belgian IPA satisfies the needs of hopheads and Belgian beer nuts alike with thick, candy-coated Belgian beer flavor mingling nicely with fresh West Coast hops to create a beautifully balanced and nuanced beer. Infidel captures the intent of a Belgian triple and the assertiveness of a West Coast IPA.

> *Selkirk's first four beers to go to market are exceptional in every respect. After Infidel, the most popular beer it sells in bottles is its rye saison, St. Stephen. A beautifully unique beer, St. Stephen has the barnyard characteristics of a saison, with grassy hops and peppery yeast esters, along with the dark bread bite of rye. White is a wonderfully refreshing wit beer with generous helpings of orange and coriander that finish the beer off nicely. Deacon is a beautiful interpretation of a Belgian pale ale with fruity aromas and a smooth, crisp finish. Coming soon is $10°$, the highly anticipated Belgian-style quad from Idaho's only abbey.*

It's those hops, and the fact that Jeff already lived there, that caused Selkirk Abbey to rise among the outlet malls and bowling alleys of Post Falls. Some of the best hops in the world grow very close to Selkirk Abbey. "Right up in Bonner we've got Elk Mountain Farms, the world's largest single hop farm. They grow some of the highest-quality hops I've ever seen," said Whitman about his neighbors in the Panhandle.

That's not all. Selkirk Abbey also takes advantage of the high-quality barley and malt that can be found right here in Idaho. "My grain is most likely Idaho grown. The wheat we use is definitely from the Palouse." Whitman continued, "I'm just very lucky that Idaho is the perfect place for brewing…For starters, our water is ideal. Here we don't do anything to our water other than filter for chlorine."

Selkirk Abbey has separated itself from the rest of the Idaho breweries by focusing on Belgian brews but makes its case as a strong Idaho brewery by offering strong, hoppy Belgian brews such as Infidel and Deacon Belgian Pale Ale. It stays true to itself by offering local patrons a wide variety of Belgian brews that can only be found on tap, either in the taproom or at one of its few accounts around the state. Those beers include the Imperial Belgian dark ale Octavian, St. Thomas Black Saison and Guilt, a Belgian-style porter. The packaging is also eye catching, and the beautiful labels make the beers appear like a top-shelf product. Each label, while having its own look, has a definitive theme that doesn't leave any doubt what brewery your twenty-two-ounce bottle came from.

Selkirk Abbey would not have been possible without the yeast it is able to buy and cultivate. The esters and other flavors that come from the yeast are critical to the success of Selkirk. "To us, it's about treating the yeast well," said Whitman about his not-so-secret ingredient. "If you treat your yeast well, it will treat you well."

GARDEN CITY BREWING NEIGHBORS

Located just northwest of downtown Boise lies Garden City, Idaho. A municipality of Ada County, Garden City is so named for the Chinese gardens that used to dot the landscape some fifty years ago. Garden City's main thoroughfare, Chinden Boulevard, is where you will find many things. It isn't a street that you would hit up on your lunch hour, as it lacks the fast-food and sandwich shops you would find on Glenwood or State Street, but it's a street you would seek out if you wanted to hide away in the Dive Bar or get your groove on at the "Worlds Famous" Ranch Club. You could buy a used car on a couple of different lots or seek out your favorite taco truck parked in one of the many strip malls. Along Chinden, which according to Donna Kahn (who wrote the book on Garden City) is an amalgamation of the words *Chinese* and *garden*, there stands an endless sea of commerce where once were beautiful gardens. As an arterial street connecting the emerging towns of Eagle and Meridian to the capital, you are much more likely to rent a storage locker or get some keys copied along Chinden now than to plow a row or plant a flower patch.

It isn't just taco trucks, dive bars and car lots along Chinden Boulevard these days, as three breweries now call Garden City home. Payette Brewing Company opened in 2010 off Chinden Boulevard, on Thirty-third Avenue in a large industrial building. Crooked Fence Brewing Company opened in February 2012 about three and a half miles down Chinden in a strip mall. Kilted Dragon opened in December 2012 just about one mile away from Crooked Fence in a small industrial park. Crooked Fence then doubled its exposure in Garden City by opening its restaurant, Barrelhouse, in June 2013. In a little over three years, what was once a street lined with gardens and then with commercial interests became home to three of the most influential breweries in Idaho.

Garden City brewers unite! Payette's Mike Francis, Kilted Dragon's Cory Matteucci and Crooked Fence's Kris Price hang out in Payette's taproom.

Chinden and Thirty-third Street in Garden City, just a block away from Payette Brewing Company, three miles away from Crooked Fence and only four miles away from Kilted Dragon.

Garden City's Brewers at a Glance

Gathering the owners of Payette, Crooked Fence and Kilted Dragon wasn't too difficult. Mike Francis, owner and brewmaster at Payette, offered up his brewery as a meeting place. At the last minute, we were able to get Kris Price, co-owner and brewer of Crooked Fence, and Cory Matteucci, co-owner and brewer of Kilted Dragon, into an office above the full taproom to sit down and talk beer. Mike was nice enough to offer up some of his tasty brews, and the conversation was on.

It was a banner day for Mike and Payette, as a recently installed twelve-head rotary canning line sat in his production room downstairs, with empty cans of North Fork begging to be filled.

North Fork Lager, a year-round beer for Payette, is a refreshing, thirst-quenching, pilsner-style lager. Noted for its low alcohol and big flavor, it quickly has become a "macro-substitute" for Idaho bars.

"I have no faith in that canning line," a usually optimistic Mike Francis offered when asked when Payette would start to put out its own cans. "I have a lot of faith in the actual canning line. It's like two and a half months late, so when I hear it's going to start tomorrow, I'm like, 'Yeah, okay.'"

Payette was among a few Pacific Northwest breweries to utilize a "mobile brewing line." The brewery pays another company to show up with its canning line, package the beer and then head off down the road. It's an unusual spot for the former industrial engineer. Before graduating from Chicago's Siebel Institute of Technology's brewing school and cutting his brewer's teeth at Seattle's Schooner Exact Brewing, Mike's path started on the 737 jumbo jet production line at Boeing, conceptualizing and building jet engines.

"I was working with people who had done it for thirty or forty years and hated it. They would complain about what they wish they'd done, so I was like, 'I'm going to go learn to brew.' So I went and did that," recalled Mike, who did just that.

Upon opening Payette, he received almost immediate praise for his beers. Outlaw IPA, Pale Ale and Mutton Buster Brown were immediate hits in the Boise market. Before long, North Fork Lager was also making inroads around town. Payette found itself in a fantastic situation for any new brewery: keeping up with massive demand.

Above: Payette owner Mike Francis and Kilted Dragon co-owner Cory Matteucci share a laugh inside Payette's taproom.

Left: North Fork Lager awaits its fate as Payette's first beer canned with its very own canning line.

*Outlaw IPA, Payette Pale Ale and Mutton Buster Brown Ale round out
Payette's year-round brews. Outlaw, a classic West Coast IPA, boasts
citrusy flavors of orange and grapefruit with a nice malt balance. Pale
Ale is an English-style pale made with crystal malts and rich, earthy
hops. Mutton Buster Brown Ale is a heavily hopped brown with hints
of brown sugar and roasted nuts to go along with piney, resinous hops.*

"Being the first production brewery helped us get where we're at because
there wasn't really much else out there. Our cans came out, and we were the
first people to get into cans. We also make some great beer, but we've been
fortunate with our timing." This is a typically modest view taken by Mike
about the rise of his brewery.

When Payette first moved into its space, one got the impression of a boy
in his father's suit. A fifteen-barrel kettle and mash tun sat at the end of a
corridor of two or three fifteen-barrel fermenters and a lone brite tank. The
bar, which was mostly tended by Mike's sister, Sheila, or Mike himself, was a
beautiful centerpiece to the taproom, which featured little else. The second
part of the building was empty, with some minor piping, showing off the
future of the brewery, poking through the ceiling. It was definitely meant to
always be a production brewery, with a strong focus on the future—the sort
of place you would think an industrial engineer would conjure up. It wasn't
too long until Payette started putting out its cans.

Payette's packaging is both eye catching and relatable to the Idaho market.
The cans sport the signature bull's-eye logo with a sort of Old West font that
is identifiable and easy to read. Each beer has its own color, with some even
showing off a little graphic. Utilizing the can format wasn't just something
that Payette did to be different; it was a conscious decision by Mike to give
Idahoans a package that they could use while playing outdoors.

"On a river," is the place Mike said is the best place to enjoy his beers, and
it's a sentiment shared by other breweries in the state. The Payette cans allow
people to take his beers out into the wilderness and even give them a target
to shoot at if there aren't any deer or elk to hunt.

The next brewery down Chinden Boulevard is marked by a green-and-
black repurposed ambulance called the "Am-Brew-Lance," which sits in
front of a fairly innocuous strip mall housing Crooked Fence Brewing
Company. In a sort of ironic twist, Crooked Fence sits inside a very plain,
sterile commercial strip mall about three and a half miles west of the
Payette brewery.

Crooked Fence Brewing and the "Am-brew-lance" on Chinden Street in Garden City.

It's ironic because Crooked Fence has perhaps the most identifiable artwork and designs of all the breweries in Idaho. The tiny taproom is filled with beautiful and interesting artwork, from the metal-worked tap handles to the T-shirts and labels designed by co-owner Kelly Knopp that decorate a space once designed for a boring dry cleaner or insurance agent.

The art extends to the brew house, where each tank has been fitted into the tight space with precision and care by the brewery's co-owner/brewer Kris Price and head brewer, Adam Dahl (who is a professional welder). "I think we take an artistic, almost rudimentary approach as far as our brewing equipment goes," stated Kris. "You walk into our brewery, and it's definitely like this shit is just thrown together. We like it that way." He added, "We're in a facility that's not built to be anywhere close to being a brewery."

A new kettle sat in the wings when I walked into the brewery. It was almost boring in its beautiful stainless steel normalcy, as what looked like a large copper balloon sat steaming next to the mash tun. Crooked Fence purchased the copper kettle from Anheuser-Busch. It was built as a showpiece and wasn't used until Crooked Fence fired it up for the first time to brew Rusty Nail Pale Ale. With a little rectangular door, complete with a handle, the kettle looks more like a hobbit home than a fifteen-barrel beer kettle. But at the time I walked in, brewer Jon Cano was stirring the wort of what would soon be Devil's Pick IPA, a popular brand for the "rudimentary" Chinden brewery.

It's inside this odd-looking kettle that Crooked Fence crafts some of its delicious, albeit odd, beers. "We're a little bit different. We don't follow guidelines by any means in the beers that we brew," said Price matter-of-factly. "We don't care."

Just because a beer doesn't follow strict Beer Judge Certification Program standards, it doesn't mean the beer isn't good or even great. Take Crooked Fence's excellent seasonal Adelaide, which is a hoppy, fresh hop brew made with Idaho's unofficial state fruit, the huckleberry. The huckleberry trade, I found out from Price, can mean some shady business to get his beer made.

"We do a huckleberry beer every year where we source local huckleberries," he started. "We buy them from some pickers out of New Meadows [just northwest of McCall]. They come down, and I do some sort of weird drug transaction for these huckleberries up in McCall. I don't really know what's going to happen. We met in a Ridley's parking lot. I parked next to his car, and he got out. He had the cooler in the back of his car. I gave him cash and then the cooler, his huckleberries move from his cooler to my cooler and he just walks away without saying anything."

Price's history suggests that more stories like this and more odd, delicious beers will be coming in the future. He started down the brewing path working at one of the local beer distributors in Boise and then moved to Fort Collins, Colorado's New Belgium as a supplier. "Going back to Fort Collins and going into the brewery and hanging out with those guys, that's where I really fell in love with beer completely," Price recalled.

It isn't out of the realm of possibility to suggest that because of Price's love of New Belgium and the artistic approach of the brewery, some interesting and fun brews will come out of that strip mall in the future. "If you kick back and put your feet up, something's wrong, man," Price said when asked about the success of his company, "I never—I don't ever look at it and say that we're successful."

Cory Matteucci, co-founder and brewer at Kilted Dragon Brewing Company, measures success three barrels at a time. Brewing on Boise's smallest system, he said about his micro-setup, "We are probably the closest to a big-size version of a home-brew system that you can get."

Kilted Dragon co-founder Cory Matteucci gets his inspiration from Dogfish Head. "I ended up reading [Dogfish Head founder Sam Castiglione's] book and realizing that he started off basically on a fifteen-gallon brew system."

Coming out of that smaller brew house are big, malty flavors. Eschewing the traditional route of most breweries, the owners of Kilted Dragon—Matteucci and partner Jeremy Canning—take great pride in not having a signature IPA or pale ale, instead focusing on the sweeter, maltier English- and Scottish-style ales that their name suggests.

Kilted Dragon's brewery and taproom sit in an industrial park just about a mile west from Crooked Fence on Chinden Boulevard. The first thing you notice when entering the sizeable taproom is just how big this small brewery seems. High up on the ceiling fly several flags—among them the Scottish blue and white cross and the royal coat of arms of Scotland, telling you exactly what you need to know about what you should order first.

Kilted Dragon, much like the other Chinden Boulevard breweries, has a completely different take on beer. Whereas Payette is geared toward tradition and Crooked Fence takes a more untraditional approach, Kilted Dragon's two brewers seem more intent on creating exciting flavors within traditional varietals. "We have focused on the 'not-IPA' of things," stated Matteucci. "Why fight the battle because Outlaw's doing well…I'm not a big hop, bitter guy, so we've focused on our porter and our amber and some of the lighter beers."

Kilted Dragon's signature beers include Bonnie Heather Amber Ale, which was quite refreshing without being too sweet; Frost Bridge Scottish Ale, a smooth, malty beer with flavors of caramel and toasted nuts, as well as just a bit of noble hop flavors; Wize Hefeweizen, a refreshing, unfiltered wheat beer; and Highland Honey Dirty Blonde Ale, brewed with honey malt. This beer has a smooth, creamy mouth feel balanced with grassy, noble hops.

Speaking with Canning and Matteucci about the beginnings of Kilted Dragon, the word "Craigslist" pops up. There's nervous laughter and an awkward silence. "We met on Craigslist," laughed Canning. It seems that they were each looking for somebody to home-brew with and found each other there.

Being the smallest brewery in Boise, in terms of barrels produced, has meant having to reshuffle the business plan a little bit for Kilted Dragon.

"When I look at the problems we have today, they are much different than what we had a year ago," Matteucci offered. "Even though we have a different set of problems, we have full kegs of beer in the cooler, we have grain in our facility and we can make some more beer. We're still struggling; it's getting better, but the problems are different."

For now, Kilted Dragon will fly on, making smooth, easy-drinking beers for the people of Garden City who aren't into big hops or giant ABVs. "I hope everybody can find their niche," said Matteucci. "Because everybody is going to be a little bit different and unique. Nobody's going to make the same beer."

A Sit Down with Garden City's Brewers

Sitting down and chatting with three brewery owners is a little bit like getting three quarterbacks from opposing teams to get together. These guys all like one another and legitimately want the best for one another, but you could sense a friendly, and healthy, competition.

"We don't hang out as much as we should," said Mike Francis of Payette with a note of sarcasm. That's because these are extremely busy people.

"I personally haven't set foot in Payette in a while, not because I don't want to but because we have been busy," explained Crooked Fence's Kris Price.

"The good news is all of us are growing, which means we're busy, but we don't have free time to hang out," Kilted Dragon's Cory Matteucci told the group. "These guys have been instrumental to Jeremy and I starting the brewery."

Apparently, choosing Garden City had less to do with the spacious views as it did with the cheap space. "Price per square foot was best off Chinden… Water cost was built into our rent," said Matteucci about why he and his partner chose Garden City.

"The rent's good. We didn't know if we were going to do any business or not. It was close to a main road so we could get trucks in and out," offered Price about why he chose the tiny Boise suburb.

"We found a good place for our production facility. Good rents, good location. I like the building more than anything else," Francis said.

Rent and price per square foot weren't the only reasons these brewers started up in Boise. With the exception of Matteucci, they were from Idaho and wanted to brew in Idaho. Matteucci came to Boise during his travels working in IT and fell in love with the city. Francis and Price, both from

Boise, saw the beauty and promise in both the city of Boise and the state of Idaho.

"Idaho's great. Garden City…it just kind of fell to what it is, as far as locations go. It is kind of centralized, which is nice. If you want people to check out your brewery from Meridian or up on the bench or wherever, its kind of a centralized location," Price said of Garden City.

"I grew up here," Francis started. "There's plenty of great places in the country to have good breweries, but I just wanted to live in Boise and make beer. We have hops forty miles away, [and the] number-one barley-growing state in the country, I just found out, which is pretty cool."

Cory Matteucci chimed in, "I was working IT and traveling across the United States. I wanted to build roots in Boise. I moved here for different reasons, and I fell in love with the city."

The conversation turns to how these three brewers actually enjoy beer. Kris Price noted, "We're in Idaho; you gotta take advantage of that. When you're fishing, when you're out there on the Salmon, steelhead fishing, right? You got a can of Outlaw in your hand or a can of Rusty Nail in your hand. It doesn't get much better than that."

Matteucci is a little bit more social about his beer drinking, especially outdoors. "Having a beer anywhere you can, it is awesome. One of my favorite places was taking it up to Montana and sharing it with a bunch of great friends around a campfire with a bunch of cigars."

These breweries are experiencing growing popularity among Idaho beer drinkers, but they wouldn't be as successful without money and recognition coming in the form of tourists. Beer geeks from Seattle, Portland and the Bay Area are starting to seek out these breweries to see what they have to offer.

"We had a bunch of people from Google in our place the other day," Price began. "They went in there, they stayed for a while, they got pretty lit and they were sort of buying up a bunch of posters and shit, and they were like, 'You're going to get a bunch of exposure; we're executives from Google.'" Price paused, as everybody chuckled at the oddity of the story. He ended the story with, "I think craft beer is one of those things that you look for—local breweries, you know."

Mike Francis added, "There are people that give the best backhanded compliments, like, 'You know, this is actually good!' And you're like, 'What were you going into this with?'" He continued, "That's part of the reason why I moved back. I think now that, over the last few years, there's great beer here. When I used to come home five years ago, people would be like, 'Yeah, Bend's got great beer,' now it's like, 'Boise's got great beer.'"

Price continued, "I agree with Mike on that. I think people are starting to realize that you can say that now—that there's good beer coming out of Idaho. It was so long that Idaho didn't have anything, so it got so easy and comfortable to say, 'Yeah, there are New Belgium and Sierra Nevada and all these huge national brands' that are something Idaho had. I think people are starting to realize we have good beer."

Part of that good Idaho beer is great ingredients, many of them coming from the Gem State. Crooked Fence doubles down on locally sourced materials for its fresh hopped huckleberry beer, Adelaide. Crooked Fence also uses malt that is at least partially grown in Idaho. Payette has taken it a step further. "These guys have a silo," Price said, motioning toward Francis. "So, Country Malt [of Pocatello], they have their bulk facility, their truck facility that's actually called Idaho Grains. Mike's getting grains I guess that are malted in Idaho." Indeed he is, as 100 percent of Payette's base malt comes from Idaho.

One thing is for certain: whatever the future holds for Idaho brewing, Chinden Boulevard has become a main artery feeding the creativity and deliciousness of Gem State beers. When Mike Francis decided to set up shop and begin packaging on Thirty-third Street off Chinden, he changed the game of Idaho brewing.

Rick Boyd, owner of Brewforia beer market and Grind restaurant, offered, "We opened, and about six months after that, Payette launched, and those two things propelled the Boise craft beer market forward by decades." He continued, "When Payette opened, it was the first brewery to open in Boise in seventeen years. Nobody had opened a brewery in the valley in seventeen years!"

Crooked Fence has expanded its operations to two suites in the same strip mall; one is the brewery, and the other acts as the offices/silk screening center for the company's creative T-shirts. It has a distributer for the state of Idaho, and you can find twelve-ounce cans, twenty-two-ounce bottles and tap handles of Crooked Fence from Sandpoint to Twin Falls.

Kilted Dragon continues to pump out quality beers in small quantities. After celebrating its one-year anniversary, Jeremy and Cory plan to keep serving up their malty craft beers to an ever-increasing group of regulars.

"Right now, I feel successful," offered Mike Francis. "But I don't think there's an end to it. With anything in life, there's never—you're just never done."

Chinden Boulevard no longer belongs to rows and rows of Chinese gardens. There is a Golden Wok Chinese restaurant located just about at Chinden and Fortieth Street, but vast fields of flowers and shrubs have given way to mostly commercial and industrial buildings. However, the ground is still as fertile as ever. Boise's upcoming beer movement may well have been planted along this offshoot street connecting the capital to its western neighbors in little Garden City, home to three of Idaho's most important breweries.

SOCKEYE BREWING HOOKS NATIONAL ATTENTION

Sockeye salmon is probably the creature most associated with the Pacific Northwest and the many rivers, creeks and streams that pass through and between Washington, Oregon, Idaho and Montana. The salmon itself, which famously swims upstream to spawn and has an uncanny ability to get back to where it was born, represents the strength, courage and willpower that most businesses, let alone breweries, won't ever achieve.

Growing up in the Northwest, catching a salmon is almost a right of passage for young anglers hoping to impress their friends or family members. It also happens to arguably be the best-tasting fish that you can find in a river. In Idaho, you have to pay an extra fee to fish for them, and they cost about five dollars more per pound than steelhead trout at a local grocery store. Sockeye are known as the toughest salmon to find. When you finally do catch a Sockeye, you don't ever forget that fishing spot and you always go back for more.

Sockeye Brewing Company, in Boise, embodies the spirit of the salmon in that it has survived through thick and thin. Kevin Mills started the original four-barrel brewery in a glorified storage unit just east of Boise. He purchased the Bavarian-style kettle and mash tun, and then looked to his friend Kevin Bolen to help brew those first beers. Kevin then went on to become the head brewer at The Ram in Boise, so in came Josh King. Sockeye experienced enough growth to move out of the storage unit and into its current brewpub on Cole and Eustick in Boise in 2002.

Sockeye Brewing Company is "Idaho Preferred." What this means is that Sockeye, whenever possible, uses Idaho-grown or Idaho-supplied ingredients in its beer and pub food. Also, 100 percent of the base malt

Sockeye brewmaster Josh King and head brewer Kevin Bolen on Sockeye's brand-new twenty-barrel brew house at the new brewery on West Fairview in Boise.

used by Sockeye comes from Great Western Malting in Pocatello, and since Sockeye has a silo, it is assured of getting grain all grown by Idaho farmers. Sockeye also has worked with local hop farmers in order to source more hops from the Gem State.

The next step in Sockeye's adventure up the stream was actually a step backward, or, as Dave Krick (owner of Bittercreek Alehouse) explained, "When Kevin started Sockeye out off of Federal Way, it took him a while to get dialed in. He worked really hard at it, and he did a nice job in the early days, but ultimately it was a struggle with that four-barrel system."

Josh brewed with Kevin Mills for ten years before the property owners, Fred and Linda Sherman, bought out Kevin in 2005. But Sockeye kept on swimming. The new owners put in a beautiful copper seven-barrel brew house and let Sockeye slowly build over the next six years on the strength of Dagger Falls IPA and Power House Porter. Josh continued to brew for the new owners at the pub.

"Fred, the property owner who had some money to be able to put some money into it, saw the potential in the industry and empowered Josh, who's a great brewer who paid his dues at The Ram, and helped Sockeye during all the frustrating lean years," Krick said of the buyout.

Dagger Falls IPA was starting to become a force around Boise, but it was only available on draft. With nobody else packaging beer in cans or bottles in the Treasure Valley, Sockeye Brewing, as described by Brewforia owner Rick Boyd, was content where it was. "Sockeye was going; it had no interest in growing."

Then something happened that Boyd said changed the beer game in Boise. Payette, the brand-new brewery off Chinden Street in Garden City, began offering twelve-ounce cans of Mutton Buster and Payette Pale in July 2012.

As with most instances of competition, the real winners were the beer drinkers of Idaho. Sockeye's owners decided that it was time to take Dagger Falls IPA, Power House Porter, Hell Diver Pale Ale and the rest of Sockeye's delicious beers to market. They made three hires that would positively change the course of the brewery, and perhaps the Boise beer scene, for the next several years when they brought in the sales team of Tylar Bell and Todd Marshall from Boise Budweiser distributor Stein Beverage, as well as rehired Kevin Bolen.

Kevin started home-brewing in 1990 back in Michigan, where he was doing construction and landscaping work between his brew days. He moved out to Boise, got a job at The Ram, was the head brewer at Sockeye for a year and then went back to The Ram, where he was the head brewer for fourteen years. He went to Grand Teton, in Victor, to brew for a year before deciding that he missed Boise. So, back he came and was welcomed with open arms by Josh, whom he helped train during their days at The Ram. Kevin came back to run the new twenty-barrel production brewery that opened in 2013.

> One of the benefits to having Kevin Bolen back in the Sockeye fold is the years of experience he brings to brewing. One of Josh King's prized aspects of his brewery is the seventy years of collective experience that Kevin and the other brewers have to draw on when brewing Sockeye beers. Said Josh, "It's just trying to figure out everybody putting their heads together and making the best beer possible."

The production brewery would make enough beer to put Sockeye in the hands of everybody in Idaho and then some. Sockeye would need to decide what to put its beer in and how to get it into the thirsty hands of people throughout Idaho. It quickly decided to put the beer into twelve-ounce cans.

The new Sockeye Brewing on West Fairview in Boise.

Born and raised in Long Beach, Sockeye sales associate Todd Marshall has a laugh in front of the brewery's oak barrels.

Tylar Bell, general sales manager at Sockeye Brewing.

Josh King explained that they went with cans because "they got a polymer lining in them that basically takes away that can flavor. It's different marketability because you can do different colors." About the flexibility of cans, Kevin added, "Having it in cans gives people that much more incentive to go enjoy it in different places. On top of the mountain, in the water, on the water—you can't take glass anywhere."

Selling the beer would be put in the capable hands of Tylar Bell and Todd Marshall. Tylar and Todd had both been reps at Stein Beverage, the local Budweiser distributor, when Sockeye approached them. For Tylar, an Idaho native, it represented a chance to take a local brewery to new heights.

Todd, a native of Long Beach, California, had really loved the craft beers of Firestone Walker, Stone, Sierra Nevada and others that he had experienced in Southern California and figured that he could teach himself to sell beer.

Sockeye pushes the boundaries of beer and of how the sales staff gets the beer out to the market. Many craft brewers prefer to distribute through what are known as "craft houses," or distributors that focus on many small breweries instead of having Budweiser, Coors or Miller in their books. Sockeye bucks the trend, choosing to go with Bud houses around Idaho. Tylar Bell said that the decision comes down to numbers: "Typically, [Bud distributors'] books are way smaller than MillerCoors houses or independent craft houses. 5,000 SKUs versus 500. You don't want to be buried in the book just to be buried in a book. You can't walk into any bar or restaurant that hasn't had Bud or Bud Light."

Sell it they did. One of the groundbreaking deals made by an Idaho brewery came in 2013, when Tylar and Todd successfully negotiated Dagger Falls IPA and Power House Porter twenty-four-packs into Costco warehouses all over Idaho. The twenty-four-packs were such a hit that they expanded to Washington State in 2014.

"I think the defining moment for this brewery was when we actually started plans for this brewery, having Kevin Bolen come back, having Todd and Tylar—that's the defining moment, really," said Josh King about the status of Sockeye Brewing moving forward.

Tylar agreed. "I have cans in the market. I have a tremendous crew all the way around with canning and brewing and our sales team. Everything is falling into place."

Sockeye's Beers: Drink Like a Fish

One of the defining characteristics of Sockeye's beers is its multicolored cans. Dagger Falls IPA is in red, Hell Diver Pale Ale orange and Power House Porter brown, and they stand out on the shelf. Sockeye has done a lot more than sell colored cans to stand out in what is becoming a very competitive statewide craft beer market. Sockeye's beers came up being the most likely to sell well on a national level when speaking to people in Idaho's craft beer business. Both fellow brewers and people on the market side of Idaho beer agree that Dagger Falls IPA could be the most marketable beer in the Gem State. It's not just that it has the hoppiest IPA (it does) or that it makes a wonderful brown porter (it does that too); it's that the beers Sockeye crafts for the mass market are consistent, clean and accessible. Dagger Falls IPA is the beer most people think about when you discuss Sockeye.

"When cans became available, because we believe in Sockeye and that beer in particular, we packaged six-packs up and sent them to the top-ten beer bars in the U.S. for free," offered Rick Boyd when asked how Idaho beers would play on the national market. "We just sent them six-packs and said, 'This is what you need to be talking about.' Something we do as a proponent of Idaho beer, when we first opened up, I went to Josh and Fred at Sockeye. I said, 'You guys need to put beer in packages for us.'"

The cans eventually came out, and now Sockeye beers are available in both Idaho and Washington. Dagger Falls IPA is an interesting "single" IPA. The first thing you notice when you crack open the can is the huge amount of citrusy hop aromas that escape out of the small opening. Pour the beer into a glass, and you'll notice its deep-orange color with a lacy white head. Aromas of Northwest-style hops—mainly Simcoe and Centennial—dominate the nose of this beer. The first sip is bitter—really bitter. Rumor was that Dagger Falls IPA, at a mere 6.5 percent alcohol by volume, was more than 100 International Bittering Units (IBUs), a number usually reserved for American-style barley wines, imperial stouts and imperial IPAs.

"It came in at 94 IBUs," Josh King said, with just a touch of facetious shame that his fabled 100 IBU IPA came in 6 units shy.

The second sip of Dagger is a beautiful thing. It's still bitter, but now that your palate has had a chance to acclimate, you get flavors of grapefruit flesh, orange rind and a little piney stickiness that allows the beer to wash over your tongue. With medium alcohol, the beer has almost no heat to take away from a touch of sweet malt that you get in addition to the big hoppy flavors that dominate the profile. It's no wonder that Dagger Falls IPA is routinely the bestselling beer in craft shops, and Costco warehouses, around the state.

Power House Porter, the second beer introduced to Costco shoppers, is a rich, chocolaty brown porter that many in Idaho prefer to the hoppy Dagger Falls. Power House brings flavors of chocolate, toffee and burnt caramel, with just a touch of hop bitterness that finishes the beer off nicely. Power House scores highly on every craft beer website because of how clean and accessible this porter truly is. There are few porters from small craft breweries that do as well as Power House does around the state of Idaho.

An important part of any Idaho brewer is its lighter side. Sockeye gets street cred for the IPAs, stouts and specialty beers, but if you want to sell a lot of beer in Idaho, you need something light. A great golden ale or light lager should be a staple for any Idaho brewer because most beer drinkers in the Gem State are macro-lager drinkers, and the large population of farmers or ranchers want something light and refreshing after a long day working the fields. Galena Gold wins on both levels; it brings subtle hoppy flavors along with the distinct characteristics found in kölsch-style beers that craft fans would appreciate. Galena Gold not only offers an olive branch of sorts to macro-lager drinkers but also allows craft beer lovers a perfect "lawnmower" beer to pair with a warm day.

Hell Diver Pale Ale is a nice complement to Dagger Falls IPA in that it is a hoppy but sweet pale ale. This Northwest-style pale has a beautiful copper color derived from some lightly roasted malts that bring a caramel sweetness and complexity that play nicely with the citrus flavors from the hops. The artwork for this beer really makes it stand out, with that "devilish" fish creeping along the river bed, ready to be snagged by a thirsty angler.

Sockeye's other year-round beers are Woolybugger Wheat and Angel Perch Amber and are not yet offered in cans. However, Woolybugger Wheat is a refreshing American-style wheat beer with subtly sour characteristics from the wheat and just a bit of grassy hops that finish the beer off nicely. Angel Perch Amber has a little more toasty malt than typical amber ales and finishes with nice bitterness. These unfiltered ales can be found on tap throughout the state.

One of the reasons for craft beer's popularity is the choice of seasonal brews that filter out as the year goes on. Sockeye's seasonal beer and barrel-aged offerings rival any in the country in terms of originality and flavor.

You can never say that Josh, Kevin and company at Sockeye are ever satisfied with one of their beers. Dagger Falls IPA has sold more than just about any other craft beer in Idaho, but these mad scientists just keep tinkering with the state's favorite IPA. Double Dagger is a wonderful double IPA that ratchets up the hops, booze and overall flavor of Dagger Falls into something completely different. These silver cans stand out, but once the beer is poured into a glass, all you get are huge, citrusy hops and heat. It's a fantastic offering and one that bitter beer lovers around the Gem State wait for every year.

Dead Dagger takes Dagger Falls into the depths of what a Cascadian or black IPA can be. To Sockeye's credit, Tylar Bell calls this beer a mix between a stout and an IPA, but I see it for what it is: a shout-out to strong American ales. Pine, bark and roasted malt dominate the nose of this beer, leading you to believe that you're getting into a thick, American-style barley wine. But the flavor is much lighter than you'd think; the roasted malts are almost driven away by piney, resinous hops and flavors of overripened fruit with a touch of currant. It's almost like the best parts of the stout and IPA used were alchemically brought to the forefront, leaving the roasted bitterness of the stout and heavy heat from the IPA behind. This beer usually makes its way to tap handles in the fall.

Speaking of the fall, Sockeye offers some of its seasonal offerings in pint-sized cans (literal sixteen-ounce cans, not figuratively "pint-sized"). Socktoberfest is a fantastic mix of sweet, roasted malts and the smooth, easy-drinking nature of a lager. The sixteen-ounce size is perfect for chatting up friends on the porch, and the beer pairs beautifully with the little bit of chill you get on an otherwise sunny fall evening in Idaho.

Winterfest, also in sixteen-ounce cans, keeps you warm and cozy on those cold Idaho winter nights. Black and crystal malt flavor give way to a surprising hop finish that gives this beer a unique character when compared to other winter warmers. The bigger can size, in addition to the greater than 7 percent alcohol by volume, means you can share this brew with a friend or have a sleepy evening with a loved one by the fire.

In the spring, Sockeye rolls out a maibock that pours a beautiful copper color with nice lacing around the glass. As found with many lagers, this maibock starts off with big flavors of ripened fruit, toffee and almonds but finishes nice and light. It's a great beer for the cool, early spring days or the warm late spring nights that you get all over Idaho.

The summer seasonal is a medium-bodied, Belgian-style summer ale called Belgian Summer Ale. Also in the big sixteen-ounce can, this beer has the clove and banana flavors derived from Belgian yeast and the smooth, malty flavor of a golden ale.

Seven Devils Imperial Stout, offered throughout the winter months, is a big, flavorful stout that pours like motor oil and drinks like a meal. By itself, Seven Devils is a nice stout, but after spending some time in whiskey and bourbon barrels, this stout really takes off. Flavors of oak char, vanilla and whiskey come out on top of the roasted malt and subtle dark chocolate flavors. If you can find barrel-aged Seven Devils, pick it up, and you'll taste just how good a Sockeye beer can be and why the motto over there is to "Drink like a fish."

THE IMPACT OF IDAHO'S BOTTLE SHOPS

The neighborhood bottle shop or alehouse—at once a modern-day comic book store, barbershop and recreation center for like-minded adults looking for a great beer. These meccas to malt are often owned and operated by people who love beer just a little bit more than their customers. Some

The classic sign hanging over Boise's oldest alehouse, Bittercreek Alehouse.

unbelievably shortsighted and embarrassingly restrictive states have made some of these places illegal, but they are now quite prevalent and varied in the state of Idaho. In fact, you can find a good craft beer bar or bottle shop in most of the Gem State's population centers. Whether you're visiting the beautiful Enoteca in Post Falls or the multifaceted Rudy's A Cook's Paradise in Twin Falls, dropping in for a pint at Bittercreek in Boise or getting a growler filled at Idaho Pour Authority in Sandpoint, chances are if you are visiting a town or city in Idaho, you can find a decent beer.

A bottle shop is much more than just a place to get a great bottle of beer. Craft beer is becoming such a "geeky" pursuit that the comic book store comparison feels more apt as people continue to switch off of macro beers and on to smaller, local craft brews. Some beers, like Epic Brewing Company's Elevated and Exponential series, are even starting to be numbered by the batch. Sierra Nevada numbers Bigfoot Barleywine by the year so collectors know what they have cellared. Collecting beers has become such a popular hobby that in the last five years, a black market has been cultivated and shut down on eBay for hard-to-find beers. Ask just about any bottle shop owner, and they will tell you (albeit reluctantly) about a friend from out of town with whom they share limited beers. Most of the time, this is a perfectly legal practice; only some states make a big deal out of people swapping local brews in the mail. Before the *X-Men* and *Iron Man* movies pushed comics to the head of popular culture, they were very much considered a niche market, perhaps even a pursuit for people whom we should say are considered short on social skills. Craft beer is no different. Words like *geek* and *nerd* are often thrown around for people heavily involved in beer. Until very recently, home-brewing was considered something that normal people just didn't do; it was even thought by many to be a dangerous pursuit.

Now we go through the retail side of the Gem State's beer community to illustrate how these carefully crafted beverages are being sold, bought and quaffed and how this important arm of the industry drives the rest of it. As you will see, the previous chapters—along with the characters and stories within them—might not have been possible without these pioneers who actually created the market for great Idaho beer.

It Had to Start Somewhere: Bittercreek Ale House

It's 1986, you're a young Dave Krick and you are helping your brother open up the (now famous) Red Door Alehouse in the emerging Fremont neighborhood of Seattle. In between pulling pints of Anchor Steam and Sierra Nevada Pale, you're sitting down next to Redhook Brewery founder Paul Shipman or having a couple of beers with *the* Widmer brothers. In other words, you are not only living during the beginning of the American craft beer movement, but you are also in the epicenter for what will become some of the most important breweries to shape the craft beer landscape, especially in the Pacific Northwest.

Let's say that you are fortunate enough to be Dave Krick and you are helping your brother start this alehouse in Seattle. But you're not from Seattle, and you want to be able to drink these wonderful new beers in your hometown of Boise. So what do you do?

You go back to Idaho with an idea for what Boise can be and how you can help shape the future of beer there, as well as, by extension, in all of Idaho. You go back to your hometown with a plan to create and maintain a downtown bar and restaurant scene to rival any in a city more isolated than any population center in the United States. You go back fired up about what you can accomplish and how you can help the people of Boise love good beer as much as you do. You quit your job at Hewlett Packard, you quit the corporate world and you gamble big on college students and Idahoans understanding that not all beer should be pale and clear. You research an area of downtown just outside the noted "party zone" of Sixth Street and opt for the recently redone Eighth Street, where you used to cruise in high school, because you can see that this will be the center of downtown Boise in the future. You find a building, the oldest in downtown Boise, because it had a cool vibe when it was a furniture store and because you like the history and interior location (corners aren't cool for alehouses; they don't have the "zen factor" that interior locations have). You want to be taken seriously, and in order to achieve that, you need to be in that old furniture building on that street during that exact time.

But if you actually are Dave Krick, you don't actually think any of these things because you just want to open an alehouse in Boise. And that's just what he did. In 1994, Bittercreek Alehouse opened on Eighth Street in downtown Boise as the first bar to offer anything but macro-lagers to residents of Idaho's capital.

"I think the craft beer business—I think we were fortunate to get into it here. We were definitely early players in it," noted the incredibly humble and soft-spoken Dave Krick, founder of Bittercreek Alehouse. "It's always been where my passion's been. But I think that if we wouldn't have done this, then somebody else would have done this like we did it in the mid-'90s. There were plenty of people seeing the craft beer scene coming on."

Maybe there were "plenty of people" who could see the craft beer scene creeping in from the West. Piper Pub opened up right before Bittercreek and had some interesting beers on tap. TableRock Brewpub, Star Garnett Brewery and Highland Hollow Brewpub were all open at the time, serving up locally made beer. What separates these places from Bittercreek is that all of them have either changed what they do, changed ownership or both. Piper Pub's website invites you to join its scotch club, with no mention of craft beers. TableRock Brewpub basically went out of business before being taken over by its landlord. Highland Hollow went through a similar transition, and Star Garnett just went out of business. So, yeah, maybe other people could see the benefit of having craft beer in Boise, but only one of them was still around to speak to me about the beginning of Idaho's craft beer scene.

"[Star Garnett] was producing good beer but not great beer. So, competing with some of the better regional breweries…the Deschutes, Sierra Nevada, Widmer…it was hard for them to compete," said Krick about the demise of Star Garnett.

Krick, in addition to starting and maintaining Bittercreek for twenty years, also had a hand in starting many of Boise's most popular restaurants, including Bardenay, Reef and the Front Door. However, his heart has always been in craft beer.

"Today, it's just Bittercreek and Red Feather [the restaurant adjoining Bittercreek]. I partnered up with a friend, and we built Bardenay and decided to take the distillery route. I liked martinis, I like gin and I like rye whiskey. The idea of doing a distillery is fun, but ultimately my passion was with beer, and I think that I always come back to Bittercreek," Krick explained about his other projects. "As we've built other restaurants and done other things, I've always found myself less happy unless the focus is on beer."

Dave Krick is all about using local ingredients, if they are of high quality. One ingredient that Idaho is known for, potatoes, was once a sore spot for Krick. "The frozen fry process is energy-intensive." Krick explained that frozen fries are blanched, cut and frozen in Idaho and then taken by freezer truck to either Los Angeles or Houston. They are taken to restaurant accounts from there, again in a freezer truck. Once they get to the restaurant, they must be kept in a freezer at -10°F. Dave uses hand-cut fries made from organic potatoes grown in nearby Hagerman. "They are cut by a human being, so we're employing somebody to do it, stored in our basement at room temperature, and they go into our fryers at room temperature, so the fryers we use today are far less energy-intensive." A novel concept—using locally sourced ingredients to save energy and money while producing a far superior product.

The focus of Bittercreek Alehouse is certainly on beer. With thirty-one continually rotating taps separated into distinctions such as "barrel aged," "Belgian strong," "hoppy," "tart" or "malty," Bittercreek's menu is perfect for the beer connoisseur and neophyte alike. What's on tap is only the beginning of what is available, as Bittercreek also offers the deepest bottle list this side of Portland.

"What we're trying to do is treat our bottle list in here much like a restaurant would treat a wine list. So we curate things that work well in that vein," said Krick about a bottle list that requires a book-like menu. "The fresh beer is all on tap. They [the bottle list] are the beers that aren't going to sell well on tap because they are higher in alcohol. For us, they are the things that, for the most part, age well because we have a deep cellar. Definitely a lot of Belgians and Germans. Most of it now, more than ever, is American beer. But it's American beer made with a particular bend that causes it to perhaps age well." He continued, "And a very small sliver of beer ages well, but when it does, we curate it into our bottle collection. Before I die, that's my goal—to have a place that people look at and say that this is the best bottle list on the planet."

Krick isn't kidding around either. Take a look inside the bottle list, and you will find four- and five-year-old Belgian trappist ales, four-year-old American sours and four-year-old verticals of various barley wines and seasonal specials. Not only that, but you will also find as many bottles from Boulevard Brewing in Kansas City as you will from Abbey de Saint Bon-Chien in Switzerland. The bottle list is impressive, and you get the feeling from Krick that he wants more. "The bottles probably represent 2 percent of the beer market, but to me they are some of the most interesting products. Most of them would be considered on the extreme side."

It hasn't been smooth sailing for Krick and Bittercreek Alehouse, as a ton of competition has popped up in the last decade or so. National big beer chain Old Chicago opened up in 1998 and ate into Krick's business for six to eight months. When Krick himself opened up Bardenay, that caused a downturn in business as well. "We kicked our ass," laughed Krick about the opening of Bardenay. "[They] did everything we did, but they did it a little bit better. And they were bigger."

One of the defining aspects of Bittercreek is the way it has evolved over the last twenty years. Every time competition has bubbled up, Bittercreek Alehouse has come out better than before. One reason is that every time a new place comes in to take Bittercreek's throne, Krick redefines the bar.

"When we opened Bardenay, it hurt bad—that's when we redid the bar," noted Krick about the nature of competition. "I knew when 10 Barrel opened…It's funny, we've been planning this remodel [they remodeled in the summer of 2013 to coincide with 10 Barrel opening around the corner] for about four years. These things have a seven- or eight-year life cycle, and then you either reinvest and up the game or get out of it. It was ironic it happened virtually the same time; in fact, we shut down at the start of remodel, I think, two or three days before 10 Barrel opened."

Krick continued, "We've been through the cycle a bunch of times. I think for us it's just the nature of the game. It's competitive. What I like about that is that it always pushes us. How will we get better? It's good for downtown Boise to have better establishments move in because none of us rest on our laurels, because if you do, you're out of here…This is a very tough business to be in, and you're only in it if you're really damn good at it. Not that we know anything more than anybody else," finished the ever-humble Krick.

Whether or not he thinks he knows more than anybody else, there has been one constant in the Boise craft beer scene over the past twenty years, and that has been Bittercreek Alehouse and its owner, Dave Krick. Others have come and gone, but Bittercreek remains and will remain for quite some time, thanks to the ever-adaptive Krick and the loyal patrons of his taproom.

Brewforia Beer Market

As quiet, contemplative and humble as Dave Krick is, Brewforia Beer Market and Grind Modern Burger Bar owner Rick Boyd is loud, boisterous and full of swagger. It's not for nothing—as much as Bittercreek has been a bedrock for Boise's craft beer scene, Boyd's Brewforia Beer Market became a catalyst for the huge steps Idaho has taken toward becoming a player in the Pacific Northwest's beer culture. Brewforia Beer Market, when it opened in the Boise suburb of Meridian in 2009, was the only committed bottle shop in the entire Boise area.

Other places, most notably the Boise Co-op, had craft bottles available for purchase, but you were more likely to find a four-star French dinner in an Idaho convenience store than you were a six-pack of craft beer.

"Our reason for existence is entirely personal frustration," started the charismatic Rick Boyd about the humble beginnings of Brewforia. "I remember the precise day. I went to the Albertsons on Seventeenth and State, and I wanted to pick up a six-pack of beer. They had nothing that I wanted. I could have the same six-pack of Sierra Pale, which I love, or a six-pack of maybe ten other pseudo craft beers and ended up buying something I didn't really want. I'm sitting there nursing a beer and thinking, 'Why doesn't somebody open a store where I can buy what I want.' That was the origination of the entire concept."

Brewforia was born! Boyd began researching what worked and what didn't within the bottle shop concept. He was fortunate enough to have a job that required travel and was able to check out similar concepts to what he wanted to do in addition to touring breweries, distributors and other retailers. This opened Boyd's eyes to the realities of alcohol laws and the differences from state to state on how beer and alcohol can be sold.

"You can't do this and you can't do that," said Boyd about those laws. "So, that was what compelled us to open. That personal frustration—it's what drives us to this day. The reason we have the website is so that we can

Brewforia/Grind Modern Burger in Eagle serving up lots of Idaho beers, including brews from Crooked Fence, Highlands Hollow and Salmon River Brewery.

make beer available to people in other parts of the country who can't get the products they want to try."

That frustration has given life to more than just a fantastic place to buy beer in Meridian, but the website Boyd refers to was a pioneering concept at the time of its launch. Anybody who wants to, provided they live in a state that allows adults to purchase alcohol online and have it shipped to their homes, can go to Brewforia.com and buy a six-pack of Sockeye Dagger Falls IPA or Payette Pale Ale and have it shipped to his or her door. In 2014, this isn't such an outlier concept, but in 2008, it was nearly unheard of.

The original Brewforia Beer Market, off I-84 in Meridian, is a wonderful place to hang out and enjoy a beer. Then, after you're done enjoying a beer (with or without food), you can pick out a few of the hundreds of bottles Boyd offers his customers. It's not just Idaho stuff, either; there is craft beer both foreign and domestic. Anything that Boyd can coax out of the local distributers ends up on his shelves, and if it ends up on his shelves, it can end up in your fridge.

Brewforia became a lynchpin for the explosion of popularity that craft beer has enjoyed in the last three years in the Boise market. Boyd calls his store "absolutely critical to the success and expansion of the market. For one, we proved there was a demand. Prior to that point, no one believed. We opened in Meridian, and we were told, 'You're going to fail massively in Meridian because everybody there is Mormon.' We've proved everyone wrong and continue to do so," said Boyd, taking a sip from an Odell Fernet Porter that he graciously shares with everybody in the bar. "We were the first that did things like samples. We made it a point to bring product in the market that did not exist in this market. We reached out to brewers."

Beer lovers in Boise can also thank Boyd for bringing beer festivals back to town. Before he even started Brewforia, Boyd had organized the Boise Beer Fest, which became the biggest beer festival in the Treasure Valley in quite some time. The first festival was in 2009, and he hasn't looked back, as each festival after that has been bigger and better than the year before.

One of the reasons for the huge success that Boyd and Brewforia have enjoyed is due to the friendly atmosphere of both of his stores. As soon as you walk in, somebody, usually Boyd, says hello and asks if you want a beer. Sounds incredibly easy, but it's not something that happens at most establishments, especially in the increasingly snobby world of craft beer.

"We underestimate the relationships that we build with people that come in and sit down at our bar. We hear it time and time again that they love coming in because they love talking to us," Boyd stated seconds after warmly greeting a couple wandering in out of the cold. "Our approach has always been to be friendly and be an educator. Never be a judgmental beer snob. You can be a beer geek, and you can be excited about beer and you can talk to people about that excitement, but you can't pass judgment."

This outlook has led to great success for Brewforia, enough that Boyd opened a second location, Grind Modern Burger, in neighboring Eagle. Grind, like Brewforia, has several rotating tap handles, as well as hundreds of bottles to enjoy at the restaurant or to take home. Unlike Brewforia, Grind has a selection of burgers that not only make for good entrées to go with the craft beers on tap but also are great enough to be considered by a local paper to be the best burgers in Boise.

"We got written up in the *Idaho Statesman* for having the best burger in the valley…by a mile," said Boyd, without a hint of false modesty. "It truly is the best burger you'll probably ever have [author's note: it is!]. A tremendous amount of thought went into producing our food."

Grind isn't just a clever name. Boyd and his team of chefs grind the patties in house everyday using a proprietary mix of beef briquette and pork belly, along with some choice seasoning, to create a burger patty that is three parts heaven and one part heart attack.

"We really wanted to up the umami factor, so we include umami-rich ingredients that are ground into the patty," Boyd proudly proclaimed about the preparation of the meat, "as well as taking things like tomatoes…the least consistent vegetable product on the planet. So, what we do is we take our tomatoes, dice them up and roast them off in our ovens to concentrate the flavors. You get a lot of umami there, plus there's umami in the meat itself, so you get this really big, bold flavor."

The big, bold flavors are needed to stand up to some of the big, bold beers that you will typically find on tap. On the two days spent researching Grind Modern Burger, I found at least two different high-alcohol or barrel-aged beers on tap, ready to enjoy (with dozens more in the cold case). The burgers themselves aren't your typical hamburger, cheeseburger or bacon burger, either, but rather are elevated to new tasting plateaus. The "plain" burger, or Modern Grind, is made with pale ale mustard, tomato confit, fresh greens, American cheese, white onions and house-cured bacon. Want something a little more adventurous in your burger? Order the DMZ with house mayo, Asian-inspired sauce and a kimchi-style slaw or reach out for the Quarter, with blackened crust, house mayo, tomato confit, red onions, fresh greens, smoked bleu cheese and house-cured bacon. All the burgers are generally priced around ten bucks and taste like a million.

If you think Boyd stopped at the burgers, then you're dead wrong. Gone are the typical French fries and in comes the modern take on the classic side. Try the Ghost Chile Fries, made with the hottest pepper on the planet and served with a house-made habanero-dipping sauce that will send you screaming for a pilsner. Try the white cheddar–bacon fries, made with house-cured bacon and white cheddar sauce and scallions; you just can't go wrong for three dollars. You could also try one of the many inspired specials that come out throughout the year.

"Idaho is kind of a unique thing, especially southwestern Idaho because we don't fall into a natural spot geographically. The rest of the Northwest doesn't consider us Northwest, [and] we're not Rocky Mountains; we're just kind of this weird amorphous island that's by itself," Boyd said when asked about Idaho on the national stage. "The beers that we produce are Northwest-style beers. The thing that makes Idaho unique [is] the opportunity to express the farm-to-glass aspect. All of the components that we associate with beer are available here. There's few places that can say that."

Customer service is still at the top of Boyd's list when it comes to the future of his shop. That means having to keep an eye out on price points and how much it costs to sit down and have a pint at the bar. "Our draft prices are probably the cheapest in town. Our package prices we try to split the difference because we're both a restaurant and retail: typically a little more than the supermarket margin and considerably less than a restaurant. That being said, we still get people who come in and say they can buy a six-pack at Albertsons for two dollars less. They don't have five hundred beers; they have fifty," pointed out Boyd as he emptied the Odell porter bottle into our two glasses. "When was the last time you went into Albertsons, and they gave you a free sample of beer?"

Bier:Thirty Moves In

Boise's east end was a collection of everything that makes Idaho's state capital great, with one huge exception: it didn't have anywhere to get a decent beer. That is, until Chris Oates, along with his wife, Kammie, decided to open up shop in the beautiful Bown Crossing Shopping Center in east Boise.

"There was nothing on the east side of town, craft beer wise, it was kind of a craft beer dead land," said Chris Oates, co-owner of Bier:Thirty. "I think it's fairly important because on this side of town, there's no representation of craft."

> Bier:Thirty started out as a Brewforia store, although it was more of a handshake agreement than an officially licensed location. Oates was the first employee at Brewforia (he worked there for two years) and decided to go out on his own, and Rick Boyd let him use the name. According to reports in the Idaho Statesman and the Boise Weekly, there wasn't so much of a falling out as there was a change in long-term goals for Chris, who wanted to offer wine and more refined food. Thus, Bier:Thirty evolved into its own place.

Chris Oates didn't really pick up an appreciation for beer until he was stationed in Korea during his stint in the military. He would drink his fair share of macro-lagers, but every so often, a Sam Adams would find him. It wasn't until after he got out of the service that his appreciation for fine beer and wine took off. His wife, Kammie, got him into wine and wine pairing dinners, and it all just sort of snowballed from there.

"Getting into wine made me start to appreciate beer and look at beer in a whole different way of actually tasting beer and tasting flavors and starting to dissect beer," Oates recalled. "Then, once you go down that wormhole, it just keeps going and going and going." At the end of that wormhole for Chris Oates was Bier:Thirty.

Bier:Thirty has a unique place in the Boise beer scene because just about any night you go in, something is going on. Woodland Empire and Edge Brewing, two breweries opening their doors in 2014, will use Bier:Thirty to "release" their beers to the public. Stone Brewing Company, Firestone Walker, Epic Brewing Company and Oskar Blues have all had hugely successful events there (and plan on having them again and again). Bier:Thirty is the place to have a brewer's event, and that's just fine with Oates.

"The events for us are really big. Where the people [are] coming in to meet the brewers, which I think is a really important thing to know the people behind your beer," said Oates. "We're the only place out here that does that kind of stuff, on this side of town. For those type of things, it's really important to have this kind of outpost for Idaho brewers. They're always welcome."

The beer events and celebrations are just part of Bier:Thirty's charm. The ever-rotating tap list and the multitude of bottle selections keep people coming back for more. Oates knows that his local clientele is just as important as the people who come in for events. "We have a few people that come in I think because of the neighborhood aspect. There are guys you see three to four times a week. Some people come in five to six times a week! We try to burn through stuff as much as possible."

"Burn through stuff" is a nice way of saying that they go through a lot of kegs. During a recent event for the newly minted Woodland Empire Ale Craft, Bier:Thirty customers drank almost thirty-five gallons of beer from that single brewery! Not to worry, though. Oates doesn't plan to run out of beer anytime soon.

"At any time, there are between thirty and forty kegs [in the cooler]," said Oates about his little keg collection that includes barrel-aged kegs and beers that he saves for special events, such as the yearly "Weekend in the Woods" event. Oates picks up and sometimes hoards barrel-aged beers from around the country and throws a big event where people can, for a small price, sample each and every beautiful oak-aged wonder.

The tap list is another passion of Oates's. You can always count on there being a couple different IPAs, a pale ale, something dark and something fun, and true to form in Idaho, a lager will always be on tap (but never a macro).

Since opening, some competition has shown up in the form of a Whole Foods store and expanded beer cases at a couple other grocery chains, but it doesn't really bother Chris, who took the Dave Krick approach and chose to fight that competition by remodeling his store. The new remodel was done to focus on the restaurant appeal of Bier:Thirty to further separate it from big-box or chain grocery stores.

"I don't want to carry everything the Albertsons down the street carries," said Oates when asked about the new look, which will bring his bottles "down" to the 400 to 450 range, all of which will be kept in coolers. "I want people to come here because they know they're going to find something they can't get at a convenience store or grocery store. A big part of us will be making the conversion from beer store to beer bar. We've noticed our business being more on-premise than off-premise just with Whole Foods opening up and Albertsons expanding their selection."

The communal aspect is also a huge part of the remodel, as capacity in the store will almost double. Instead of having tables for one or two couples, Chris has installed larger tables to fit more people in, while also increasing the interaction between his customers. Oates is hoping that this means his like-minded regulars will soon become friends. "We really like to see that, that aspect of community and neighbors."

As the name suggests, Bier:Thirty does new things in Boise in sort of an old-world way—constant events that bring people together to celebrate with beer, frequently changing tap handles of locally brewed beer and now communal tables being set up so neighbors can become friends. All of this makes Bier:Thirty more than another beer store; it's a true neighborhood pub.

Great Bottle Shops in Outlaying Areas

Brewforia is no longer the only bottle shop or beer market in the state. Since Rick Boyd opened the doors on his first Meridian location, bottle shops began popping up all over the Gem State. In what is becoming the craft beer capital of the Panhandle, Post Falls now has the wonderful Enoteca Fine Wine and Spirits shop to host beer pairings, pint nights and beer festivals for the good people of the north. In the southeast, people from Victor to Pocatello frequent MarCellar's Vintage Wines & Brews in downtown Idaho Falls.

With stores in Nampa and Boise, craft brew fans and home-brewers alike have a wonderful place to go for everything either one of them would ever want at Brewer's Haven.

The Magic Valley, found between Burley to the east and Hagerman to the west (roughly ninety miles), is served by one bottle shop: Rudy's A Cook's Paradise in historic downtown Twin Falls. Rudy's is truly a cook's paradise, as it offers cooking gadgets, specialty spices and herbs, exotic coffees and teas, glassware, flatware, table settings and a large selection of fine wines and beers.

Natalie Steele, who runs the beer shelf for Rudy's A Cook's Paradise, has been living, and drinking, in Twin Falls for pretty much her whole life. She went to Mugger's brewpub on her twenty-first birthday and worked a waitress job at Trail Creek Brewery. She has had her finger on the pulse of Magic Valley's beer scene ever since. "We try to stay informed, and we try to keep current seasonal products in," Natalie said about her current post at Rudy's. "It is actually the oldest building in Twin Falls."

To serve the thirsty residents of Magic Valley, she has to make sure that craft beer fans from Burley have a reason to trek all the way to downtown

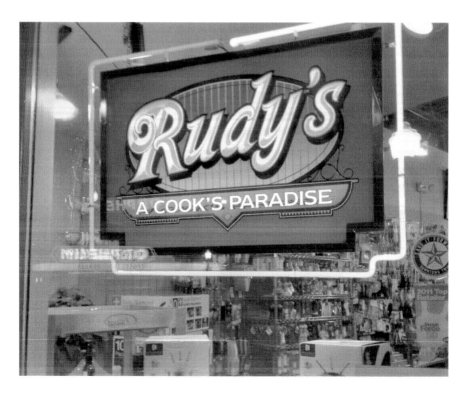

Magic Valley's source for craft beer bottles and cans, Rudy's A Cook's Paradise in downtown Twin Falls.

Twin Falls. One of Natalie's hardest jobs is making sure that what she carries at her store can't be found at the local grocery store or gas station on Highway 30.

"Imports, a lot of German, a few Scottish, local stuff too," she said, describing what she carries. "We really like Idaho beers. We like to push Idaho beers, and hopefully their craft gets better and better."

NEW BREWERIES ON THE BLOCK

The emerging Idaho beer scene would be nothing without new blood. Whether a brewery succeeds or fails, each new brewery that opens up expands the state's brewing map by that much. If Bi-Plane Brewing never opens and experiences a modicum of success, then maybe Jeff Whitman doesn't ever look at the Post Falls area as being a viable place for an all-Belgian brewery. On the flip side of that, if Coeur d'Alene Brewing Company was never forced out of its location downtown, then maybe Trickster Brewing doesn't decide to open up on the other side of town. Regardless of how the butterfly flaps its wings, each and every brewery that has come and gone has helped move Idaho's brewing community forward. Whenever a brewery fails, for whatever reason, it makes room in the Idaho market for another brewery to open up. That is no longer the case.

"The thing I would stress is that startups need to temper their ambitions and focus on a core of three to five year-round beers," said Brewforia owner Rick Boyd about the new breweries. "I know selling four or five beers every day may not be sexy, but in the long run, that's the base of your business."

Boyd knows what he's talking about. He's taken Brewforia from a tiny single store in Meridian to two big stores, including an award-winning burger and beer joint. He also knows a thing or two about selling beer in Idaho. "Perfect those core beers before attempting to spread out to seasonals, special releases, collaborations, etc. There is no point in having ninety beers in your portfolio if you don't do them all very well."

Either way they do it, new breweries are welcome with open arms to the Gem State. Nearly every brewery I interviewed said that they would welcome a new brewer with open arms, with one single caveat: "I just hope they're going to make good beer," noted Sockeye head brewer

Kevin Bolen. "If a group of people just go to that one spot that's not making good beer, then they're just going to assume that maybe there's just no good beer in Boise."

"Awesome. The biggest thing with new breweries coming in is that not every brewery is the same," said Payette owner Mike Francis. "We're all vastly different breweries. Cloud 9's [a nano brewery] going to open up, and they're more similar to [Kilted Dragon, another nano], but it's a pub, so they're really different. I'm like, 'Does a Mexican restaurant get mad that there's a pizza joint opening up next door?'"

"I'm all for it, man," said Kris Price of Crooked Fence. "I get excited to get into those breweries and check out how they run their glycol lines or the way they're going to do this or do that. I enjoy that." Price had a chance to help Edge Brewing Company lay out its new brew house, which is located in an industrial park in west Boise. That brewery, which started business in January 2014, is a fantastic example of a new brewery looking to make a splash in the Boise craft beer market.

Edge Brewing Company

Tucked away in an industrial complex just off Franklin Street near the I-184 by the Westgate Shopping Center in west Boise sits a large building where the principals of one of Idaho's most anticipated new breweries are meeting in a cold room. Going down a frigid hallway, there is one closed door that I knock on before entering. I'm greeted by a female voice, talking about shoes. "They're steel-toed, chemical-proof brewing boots, but they're pink!" explained head brewer Kerry Caldwell to her male business partners.

> *Kerry Caldwell's first head brewer experience came at the oldest brewpub in Boise, TableRock. While her time there was relatively short, she was able to show off some serious skills in the beers and meads that she was able to craft. Before TableRock, she brewed at Belmont Brewing in Long Beach, California. Belmont is an award-winning brewpub on the shores of the Pacific Ocean known for its flavorful beer and food, making Caldwell perfect for Edge. "I never thought I was going to be a brewer, and the only reason I did is because I hung out in breweries so much that one finally offered me a job!" laughed the affable Caldwell.*

BOISE, IDAHO

Edge Brewing Company's logo.

Edge Brewing Company has invested more than just pink boots in its head brewer. Edge has plans that go beyond steel toes, caustic cleanser and the color of boots that its brewer or her assistant, Tyler Evans, chooses to wear when brewing beers on its shiny new fifteen-barrel brewing system. The name "Edge" doesn't just refer to its proximity to the city limits of Boise but also to the radical approach the company plans to take when entering the market in 2014. On the business end, it has several partners who each own shares of the whole brewery. Each share cost the investors $7,500.

On the brewing side, they plan to be on the cutting edge of brewing by offering a series of one-off and seasonal brews throughout the year. "When people have a flagship beer, it robs them of growth," said co-founder Marcus Bezuhly. "If people are expecting just that one product all the time, it really kind of locks you into not being creative."

Tyler Evans, also an invested shareholder, agreed. "We hope to be making lots of different beers."

Edge Brewing is located in a giant warehouse building that has been divided up for Marcus's two companies, Edge Brewing and Homebrew Stuff. "Basically, we were looking to expand," said Marcus about the building. "So, we had found this building, and it's pretty big [fourteen thousand square feet]. *We bought it with the intent to move Homebrew Stuff into here." Instead, he decided to start a brewery this year.*

Caldwell added that one of her former breweries, Belmont Brewing in Long Beach, California, "doesn't have a house IPA, so I got to brew an IPA every week! I think we'll let the consumers decide what the flagship beer will be."

So while Caldwell is invested monetarily in Edge Brewing, its many investors have much more on the line with Caldwell. In addition to the many seasonal and one-off brews that she will be responsible for brewing, each one of the twenty-one individual investors can get time to brew a beer they want either on the twenty-gallon pilot system or on the fifteen-barrel professional brewing system. This means that Caldwell could be responsible for more beers this first year than any other brewery in Boise. To say she's up to the challenge would be selling her short. "We're going to have twenty taps that are all house beers. I plan on doing at least one seasonal tap every month," she said excitedly. "I've already gone through the calendar and found at least one real holiday [per month]. I'm going to do an organic hemp ale for Earth Day!"

Edge Brewing's co-founders feel like they have the edge when it comes to succeeding in the competitive Boise beer business. This confidence can be directly related to Marcus Bezuhly's first business: the wildly successful Homebrew Stuff home-brew supply store. "I've been in the business for about four years. My wife and I started the home-brew supply in our garage, and pretty much it just took off. We've gone from basically just my wife to twenty-three employees," said Bezuhly about his company's rise. "We're already in the business, we already have hop contracts [and] we already have associations with brewer supply group and Great Western Malting."

In other words, Edge Brewing is already ready to roll, and Marcus wants the rest of Boise's beer scene to understand that Edge isn't being built to fail. This means that Edge didn't take any chances of starting off too small. With the already-installed fifteen-barrel brew house, complete with a handful of fermenters and two brite tanks, Edge Brewing will be able to hit the ground running and also have the ability to make the "big beers" that Caldwell and her assistant Evans want to brew.

"The nice thing about our system is that we have a fifteen-barrel boil kettle, a twenty-barrel mash tun and a twenty-five-barrel hot liquor tank," said Evans. "We don't want to be stuck in having to do a half batch because we want to do a huge beer."

Marcus Bezuhly started Homebrew Stuff with his wife as an online store run out of his garage. Today, he has a hugely successful store on Chinden Street and has just opened a brewery to rave reviews. It all started as he grew up in Northern California, where his friend's dad owned Nevada City Brewing Company and his uncle owned Truckee River Brewing Company. A young Marcus would help clean up the breweries during the weekends and get a case of beer. He then learned to home-brew, and the rest is history.

It's not just a saying around Edge Brewing. Sitting in the cavernous warehouse area is a huge stack of beautiful oak barrels. The stack is made up of sixteen bourbon and eight syrah barrels sitting there in plastic, begging to be filled with beer.

"We are co-op-ing a canning line with Crooked Fence," Bezuhly said, saving this bit of information for last. "It's been built and should be shipping very soon. It's a three-head canning machine that will be set up on a trailer so it can move."

So, in its first year, Edge Brewing plans on brewing a bunch of new beers, starting a sour barrel–aging program, doing huge beers and canning whatever it is it's going to make with that giant fifteen-barrel brewing system. Sounds pretty ambitious. That's exactly what Marcus Bezuhly wants. "That's one of the reasons we wanted to come in guns a-blazing. There's some small operations—it would be easy to get lost in the shuffle unless you come in and say, 'Pay attention to us!'"

Edge Brewing is going into this the same way most of Idaho's breweries are succeeding—by using ingredients grown in and around Idaho. They are sourcing their grain from Great Western Malting and are contracting hops from Alpha Hops in Parma. Much like other breweries, Edge plans to someday brew a 100 percent Idaho beer made from locally sourced grain and hops.

The brain trust at Edge Brewing Company. *Left to right*: Tyler Evans, Marcus Bezuhly and Kerry Caldwell standing in front of their new brew house.

In the restaurant, they will be sourcing as much local meat and produce as possible. They will also be sourcing beer to use in the food that will come from their own brew house by brewing kitchen-specific beer. "For us, coming in, we want to set the bar pretty high for ourselves," Marcus said. "We want to push ourselves. Push the limits of our knowledge and our creativity and try to be unique. The best product we have to sell is our hard work and creativity."

Slanted Rock Brewing Company

Slanted Rock Brewing, in the Boise suburb of Meridian, is also jumping right into the packaging arena, but it's moving in with four flagship beers.

Initial Point IPA is a fruity, West Coast pale ale that has wonderful hop aromas with just a touch of malt sweetness. Iron Butt Red Ale is a sweet, malty amber ale with nice hop bitterness, and Silhouette Dark Ale is a smooth, brown porter with light bitterness and delicate chocolate and coffee flavors. Finally, Afternoon Delight—a light golden ale—is the bridge beer for macro-lager drinkers who pop in to Slanted Rock's taproom. These four beers make up the backbone to Slanted Rock and are the beers that owner Bob Lonseth hope will separate his new brewery from the rest.

"I was a software engineer and a brewmaster," said Lonseth. "It's a classic double threat. The business looked like fun." Located in a strip mall in Meridian, Lonseth opened his brewery after impressing his friends and neighbors with his wonderful home-brews and the belief that great beers can be made from the freshest ingredients. "Our motto is 'The Simple Elegance of Beer,'" he noted.

Slanted Rock Brewing Company unknowingly has taken Rick Boyd's advice in sticking with a core set of beers. The "core four" beers are augmented by an array of seasonal brews that include a Scotch ale, a rye beer, a wit beer and an Oktoberfest, along with a few stronger dark ales.

Another slant on the common brewery that Slanted Rock has planned is to support the community that supports the brewery. "I personally take pride in fulfilling a need in the community and supporting local and national charity," said Lonseth. That doesn't mean stuffy luncheons and fundraisers for Slanted Rock. For example, in February, website visitors were asked to support Boise's inaugural "Cupid's Undie Run" to raise money for Children's Tumor Foundation.

Slanted Rock has come out swinging in the Idaho beer market, where you can find six-pack cans of its Initial Point IPA in grocery stores and on tap around the state. This initial run has produced positive feelings in the Meridian brewery, as Lonseth has plans for expanding into his own building, saying that the definition of success will be "when we build our own site. It's in the plan!"

Woodland Empire Ale Craft

Another highly anticipated new brewery that opened up in January 2014 is Woodland Empire Ale Craft. Located on Front Street near downtown Boise, Woodland was started by Rob and Keely Landerman, who came up from Austin, Texas, to open a brewery in Idaho. It was a homecoming for company president Rob, who grew up in Idaho, and a chance for Keely, the head brewer, to show of her brewing prowess.

Woodland Empire, maybe in the hopes of creating an actual brewing empire, is also starting out with a big brew house, having fired up a fifteen-barrel system in a huge nine-thousand-square-foot building. The tasting room, which is about two thousand square feet, will have a different atmosphere than most of the other taprooms around town. There are no televisions, a bunch of couches, wireless Internet and a vibe that suggests it might be more suited to being a coffeehouse than a brewery.

Woodland Empire is hoping that you won't need to be distracted by a Boise State Bronco football game to have an excuse to come into its taproom; rather, it hopes you come to enjoy the interesting, unique beers that it has to offer.

In the Morning, a light-bodied, big-flavor English session ale, has all the subtle nuances of a mild ale but without the alcohol. The light-roasted malt flavors and subtle hop bitterness might make this more of a brunch beer than a morning beer, but the ABV, below 4 percent, suggests that brewer Landerman wanted to show off a sense of subtlety in her first set of beers.

For all the subtlety of In the Morning, Gold Days Belgian-style triple ale is an in-your-face beer with plenty of alcohol and Belgian beer flavors. Brewed with Belgian yeast and plenty of malt, this beer has wonderful cotton candy, banana and clove flavors, with a clean bitterness and very little heat for a 9 percent beer. It only gets better as it warms up, with subtle hay and grass flavors shining through the sweet malt and floral yeast.

Going back to the English-style well, Woodland has also put out an ESB called Rabbit Fighter. This crowd pleaser has been a favorite with online beer reviewers for its smooth flavor and light bitterness. A very refreshing ESB at only 5.3 percent ABV and just 35 IBUs, this beer won't fight your taste buds as it uses only two grains and a single hop variety.

Last, but certainly not least, is the all-important opening IPA, City of Trees. The hops really shine through in this beer with wonderful pine and citrus notes that go nicely with the light cracker malt. At only 6.2 percent ABV, you can have a few of these Trees and not be left out on a limb.

Other local brewers are excited about what Woodland Empire will bring in the future. Kris Price, co-owner at Crooked Fence Brewing, said, "Woodland's going to bring something different to the table, which is cool, and I'm looking forward to seeing different things."

Crowd-Funded New Breweries Cloud 9 Nanopub and Bogus Brewing

Whereas Edge Brewing Company targeted and attained shared investors while Slanted Rock and Woodland Empire self-funded their endeavors, now you have breweries looking toward the Internet and crowd-funding to attain their dream breweries. Two new breweries in Idaho went to the people through websites like Kickstarter to raise the hundreds of thousands of dollars needed to start a brewery. Through these means, the owners of these two breweries were able to get the funding they needed without necessarily carrying any outstanding debt. They give up something, too, as these investors are often promised things that could be hard for these fledgling breweries to fulfill. Only time will tell if this is a brilliant method of building a business, or if these two outliers will come up short of expectations.

Cloud 9 Nanopub (Boise's first nanopub), which was opened in the winter of 2013 by Jake and Maggie Lake, plans to focus on its outside interests of sustainability, being ecologically and environmentally friendly and proving that organic brewing can be a sustainable force in the industry.

"There are many reasons, from the ever-evolving strains of bacteria that are becoming immune to medicine, to soil health and ecology," explained Jake Lake about why his brewery is going all-organic. "We are proud to be the first and only certified organic brewery in the state of Idaho supporting local industry and small business."

Cloud 9, as a four-barrel nanobrewery, is fairly limited in the amount of beer it can produce, but that hasn't stopped the brewers from producing a large selection of beers. Only open for a few months, Cloud 9 has put out an impressive dozen beers. They aren't your typical pale ales, porters or cream ales, either, but rather ambitious fruit beers (Blackberry Blonde Ale, Huckleberry Stout), flavored dark beers (Chocolate Bar Porter, Salted Caramel Stout) and other interesting brews (Honey Basil Ale, Bourbon Oak Stock Ale) that prove that Cloud 9 isn't going to shy away from the strange or delicious just because it brews with organic materials. "We feel the taste and quality of organic products are far superior and more nutrient dense than their nonorganic counterparts," said Lake.

This doesn't mean that Cloud 9 isn't offering the standard fare of IPAs, porters and light ales. Other than the year-round Salted Caramel Stout, the rest of Cloud 9's core beers sound rather normal. However, the wit, pale ale, Northwest Red Ale, double IPA and Pinup Porter all stand out on their own as being some of the only organic beers made in Idaho. The double IPA, in particular, is an ambitious beer with more than 8 percent ABV and 90 IBU; this beer is brewed in the spirit of a Dogfish Head 90 Minute IPA in that it is a continuously hopped IPA. Cloud 9 throws generous amounts of Columbus, Centennial and Magnum hops into the boil, plus two dry-hop additions during fermentation, giving this beer more bitterness that just about any other Boise beer.

The food takes on a different tone. As outlandish as the beers sound, the food is downright traditional. With items such as mac and cheese, chicken pot pie and an assortment of salads, burgers and appetizers, the food sort of brings you back down from the big flavors being displayed by the beers.

The term *nano* doesn't just refer to the custom-built four-barrel brew house but also to the size of the brewery itself. Where Edge boasts 9,000 cavernous square feet, Cloud 9 will be squeezing its brewery, restaurant and kitchen into 1,400 square feet, roughly the size of a two-bedroom apartment. "Our entire kitchen, brewery and dining area will all fit inside the walk-in cooler of Edge!" joked Lake.

It remains to be seen whether this Kickstarter baby will grow into a healthy brewery, with its organic beers leaving Idaho beer drinkers on "cloud nine," or if the lack of brewing power will burst its bubble before it can reach the skies.

Bogus Brewing, slated to open in the spring of 2014, is another crowd-funded operation that gathered its money by the more traditional method of asking for it. Shares started at just $1,000 and include voting rights, a mug, Community Supported Brewery membership, dividends (when profitable) and the opportunity to attend what they call "Guinea Pig Nights" where you, a part-owner, get to try out beta-tested beers. The monetary commitment can be as much as $50,000. As of this writing, Bogus Brewing's crowd-funding was highly successful, with 171 owners and more than $350,000 raised.

The other component of Bogus Brewing is flexibility. Bogus's brain trust—chief brewing officer Collin Rudeen and head brewer Lance Chavez—also went big with a fifteen-barrel system that will supply its taproom and a future bottling plan. The system will support three core beers, along with the beers being produced by a series of "tenant brewers" that will be a part of a "brewery incubator" program designed to take investors and turn them into brewers. The first tenant brewer will be Dave Krick, owner of Bittercreek Alehouse, and he will have the chance to brew not just once but several times on Bogus's system. It's something that Krick has wanted to do for a long time. "Thirty-years after I decided to make beer, I'm still asking my wife when I can make beer at a commercial level. I even went to school for it," Krick told me before his involvement in Bogus Brewing.

Bogus Brewing does have one specialty under its sleeve, as it claims that it will be Boise's first brewery to focus on doing Belgian saison-style ales.

Will this new crowd-funded brewery, which will sport many different brewers and focus on Belgian-style saisons, be an excellent adventure or a "bogus brewing" journey for Idaho's beer scene? It seems that at least one Boise beer heavyweight believes in this startup, and we can only hope that Dave Krick's track record of success extends to Bogus Brewing.

LAST CALL

THE NEXT GEMS FROM IDAHO

Idaho's craft beer community began life as the love child born from the Bend (Oregon) and Fort Collins (Colorado) beer communities because that's the craft beer that was available in Idaho before Grand Teton started packaging.

Every established brewery that was interviewed for this book that distributes in cans or bottles is growing. Payette and Crooked Fence both have their own canning lines (although Crooked Fence is sharing its line with Edge Brewing); Grand Teton now brews on the state's biggest system (at thirty barrels), has added more fermentation capacity and has expanded its bottling operation; and Sockeye has moved into a brand-new facility that, at twenty barrels, is the second-largest brew house in the state. Even the smaller breweries putting out twenty-two-ounce bottles, like McCall Brewing Company and Sawtooth Brewing, are expanding to canning lines and larger brew houses. Sawtooth Brewery, after being open just two years, is now looking to move on from its one-barrel system, plus contract-brewing to its own fifteen-barrel brew house. This hasn't happened by accident. Idaho breweries are making some really good beers that Idaho craft beer lovers are drinking up as quickly as they can get them.

In other words, Idaho beer is getting to be very good, and people around the country are starting to take notice. As a last call for this book, I will offer the ten Idaho beers that you should try as soon as possible, and maybe you will find out what craft beer fans here have known for a while: they make some damn good beer in the Gem State.

10. GRAND TETON 208 SESSION ALE
The only beer made with 100 percent Idaho ingredients.

9. LAUGHING DOG ALPHA DOG IMPERIAL IPA
Citrus on the nose and piney on the tongue, with a resinous mouth feel and just a bit of heat from the alcohol. A great Imperial IPA that you can tell is brewed by a man obsessed with hops.

8. SAWTOOTH FREEHEELER RYE IPA
Ketchum's favorite beer! Bright, fresh hops with a nice bite of rye.

7. CROOKED FENCE SINS OF OUR FATHERS IMPERIAL STOUT
A rich stout with bits of coffee, roasted malt and burnt sugar flavors. Bonus points for barrel-aged, which adds a really nice vanilla flavor from the oak.

6. MCCALL BREWING WOBBILY MAN SCOTTISH ALE
Caramel, crystal malts and earthy whiskey flavors, with a fresh bitterness, make this Scottish ale a favorite for people across the state.

5. LAUGHING DOG THE DOGFATHER IMPERIAL STOUT
Smooth like silk, with over-ripened fruit and chocolate overtones kissed with bourbon. Deeply kissed.

4. PAYETTE OUTLAW IPA

A West Coast IPA separated by its grapefruit and orange flavors with a sweet malt backbone. Also, this was the first IPA canned in Idaho.

3. GRAND TETON BITCH CREEK ESB

The quintessential Pacific Northwest beer made with Idaho grains and northwest hops. One of the first commercial hoppy brown ales, Bitch Creek has inspired craft brewers from Delaware to California.

2. SOCKEYE DAGGER FALLS IPA

Boise's most famous IPA is the number-one beer mentioned by other Idaho brewers when asked what beer from Idaho would sell nationally. This beer comes at you like a hurricane of hops with no eye, hitting your mouth with enough hops to blow away your taste buds. Dagger also gets points for being the best deal in craft beer, with twenty-four-packs at Costco going for only $24.99.

1. SELKIRK ABBEY THE INFIDEL BELGIAN IPA

Selkirk Abbey is the number-one brewery that other Idaho brewers mentioned when asked which brewery could sell on the national market. Selkirk's best-bottled offering, the Infidel IPA, has a host of floral and fruity hoppy flavors married with sweet notes of Belgian malts and yeast.

APPENDIX

IDAHO'S BREWERIES
TO 1960

Brewery Name	Location	Open Dates
Albion Brewery & Saloon	Albion	1888–1893
Wilmer & Motlow Brewery	Atlanta	1878–1879
J.H. Casey Brewery	Atlanta	1886–1887
Nelson Davis Brewery	Atlanta	1886–1890
Guldorff or Gindroff Brewery	Bay Horse	1886–1887
Farnsworth & Company Brewery	Bellevue	1882
Anton Spielman Brewery	Bellevue	1882–1887
Idaho Brewery	Bellevue	1887–1890
Pioneer Bottling & Soda Company	Bellevue	1888–1891
Aug. A. Fischer Brewery	Bellevue	1890–1892
Central Brewery & Bakery	Boise	unknown–1865
Adolph & Lemp Brewery	Boise	unknown–1866
Boise Brewery	Boise	unknown–1866
Boise Brewery	Boise	1863–1907
Peter Sturzenacker Brewery	Boise	1866

Brewery Name	Location	Open Dates
City Brewery	Boise	1867
John Krall Brewery	Boise	1867–1875
Lemp & Sturzenacker Brewery	Boise	1868
City Brewery Saloon	Boise	1870
Joseph Misseld Brewery	Boise	1874–1875
John Broadbeck Brewery	Boise	1875–1900
Idaho Brewing Company	Boise	1900–1906
Idaho Brewing & Malting Company	Boise	1906–1916
L.P. Grunbaum Brewery	Boise	1910–1911
Bohemian Breweries Inc.	Boise	1933–1956
Bohemian Breweries Inc.	Boise	1956–1960
Golden Gate Brewery	Bonanza City	1878–1884
Michael Spahn Brewery	Bonanza City	1880–1891
City Brewery	Buena Vista Bar	1863–1865
California Brewery	Buena Vista Bar	1865
Centerville Brewery	Centerville	1865–1875
Fred Albiez Ferdinand Klug and George Fuchs Brewery	Challis	1879–1886
Koeninger Bros & Co Brewery	Clayton	1889–1895
Kopp & Koeninger Brewery	Clayton	1896–1899
Koeninger & Fantino Brewery	Clayton	1899–1900
Herman Koeninger Brewery	Clayton	1900–1903
Henry Reininger Brewery	Coeur d'Alene	1889–1890
Coeur d'Alene Brewing Company	Coeur d'Alene	1908–1909
Panhandle Brewing Company	Coeur d'Alene	1912–1915
Schober & Hendricks Brewery	Cottonwood	1896–1897
Cottonwood Brewery	Cottonwood	1897–1903

Brewery Name	Location	Open Dates
St. Albert's Brewery	Cottonwood	1905–1910
George Winckler Brewery	Council Valley	1886–1887
Star Brewery Saloon	Custer City	1880–1882
Pioneer Brewery	Custer City	1880–1884
Delta Brewing Company	Delta	1886–1887
Sylvester Werneth Brewery	Franklin	1884–1890
Joseph Geiger & Matt Kambitsch Brewery	Genesee	1889–1902
Genesee Brewery	Genesee	1902–1909
Hogl Demont & Kern Brewery	Gibbonsville	1895–1898
Robert Demont & George Kern Brewery	Gibbonsville	1898–1906
Eagle Brewery	Grangeville	1887–1892
Von Berge & Company Brewery	Grangeville	1892–1908
Grangeville Brewing & Malting Company	Grangeville	1899–1905
Grangeville Brewing Company Ltd.	Grangeville	1905–1910
William Von Berge Brewery	Grangeville	1908–1910
Idaho Brewery	Grangeville	1910–1915
George Miller & George Gooding Brewery	Granite Creek	1870
St. Louis Brewery	Hailey	1880–1882
George W. Kohlepp Brewery	Hailey	1881–1887
Mrs. Agnes E. Vorberg Brewery	Hailey	1882–1884
Star Brewery	Hailey	1885–1915
Hump Brewing Company	Hump	1905
Harvey & Eggleston Brewery	Hailey	1906–1910
Hailey Brewery	Hailey	1907–1910
Idaho Brewery & Bakery	Idaho City	1863–1864

Brewery Name	Location	Open Dates
Marks Knauer & Company Brewery	Idaho City	1863–1864
Coray & Pefferlee Coray & Company Brewery	Idaho City	1864
Pacific Brewery	Idaho City	1864–1865
Centerville Brewery	Idaho City	1865–1866
Miners Brewer & Bakery	Idaho City	1865–1867
Idaho Brewery	Idaho City	1865–1868
Alois Riid Brewery	Idaho City	1866–1867
Keiffer & Benegard Brewery	Idaho City	1867–1868
Haug & Broadbeck Brewery	Idaho City	1868
Riid & Broadbeck Brewery	Idaho City	1869
Nicholas Haug Brewery	Idaho City	1874–1884
Mary Haug Brewery	Idaho City	1884–1890
John Rost Brewery	Idaho City	1890–1891
Rost & Rood Brewery	Idaho City	1891–1897
Maynard & McGill Brewery	Idaho City	1892–1892
Hancock & Wilmer Brewery	Idaho City	1900
Wm. H. Thomas Brewery	Idaho Falls	unknown–1888
Kremer & Edwards Brewery	Idaho Falls	unknown–1895
Heath & Keefer Brewery	Idaho Falls	1882–1890
M. Weimann Brewery	Idaho Falls	1888–1893
Eagle Rock Brewery	Idaho Falls	1889–1890
Kurt Brewing Company	Idaho Falls	1895
Bannock Brewing Company Ltd.	Idaho Falls	1895–1907
Blum & Company Brewing Company	Idaho Falls	1896
Eagle Rock Brewery	Idaho Falls	1897–1899
Idaho Falls Brewing Company	Idaho Falls	1904–1910
Pilsner Brewing Company of Idaho Falls	Idaho Falls	1935–1937

Brewery Name	Location	Open Dates
Idaho Falls Brewing Company	Idaho Falls	1937–1939
Frank & Gundorf Brewery	Jordan Creek	1878–1879
Jacob Howarth Brewery	Juliaetta	1891–1893
Juliaetta Brewing Company	Juliaetta	1891–1893
Milwaukee Brewing Company	Juliaetta	1893–1895
Howarth & McGlynn Brewery	Juliaetta	1897–1898
Milwaukee Brewery	Juliaetta	1899–1904
Leadville Brewery Saloon	Ketchum	1881–1889
Schaeffer & Hildebrandt Brewery	Ketchum	1882
Robert Koeniger Brewery	Ketchum	1884–1902
Brown & Godfrey Gamble Brewery	Lewiston	1862
Gambel & Ernest Weisgerber Brewery	Lewiston	1862
Ernest Weisgerber Brewery	Lewiston	1862–1869
Brown & Weisgerber Brewery	Lewiston	1863
City Brewery	Lewiston	1864
California Brewery & Bakery	Lewiston	1865
Ernest John & Christe Weisgerber Brewery	Lewiston	1869–1871
John & Christe Weisgerber Brewery	Lewiston	1871–1889
Christe Weisgerber Brewery	Lewiston	1889–1912
Lewiston Brewing Company	Lewiston	1933
A.W. Vanderwood Brewery	Malad City	1884
W.G. Jenkins Brewery	Malad City	1886–1887
Blume & Dill Brewery	Malad City	1889–1890
John Herman Brewery	McAuley	1889–1890
Fries & Company Brewery	Moscow	1882–1886
Joseph Niederstadt Brewery	Moscow	1886–1890
Niederstadt & Schober Brewery	Moscow	1890

Brewery Name	Location	Open Dates
Niederstadt Schober & Koehler Brewery	Moscow	1891–1894
Moscow Brewery	Moscow	1895–1901
Herman Nicola Brewery	Moscow	1902
Moscow Brewery	Moscow	1902–1908
Jacob & John Lemp Brewery	Mountain Home	1874–1875
Carl Mallon Brewery	Murray	1884–1888
Rammelmeyer & Seelig Brewery	Murray	1886–1887
Ernest Rammelmeyer Brewery	Murray	1887–1888
Crescent Brewing Company	Nampa	1906–1916
Overland Beverage Company Inc.	Nampa	1934–1950
F.K. Walker Brewery	Oxford	1886–1887
Stirm & Miller Brewery	Payette	1888–1889
Stirm & Hoffman Brewery	Payette	1889–1890
W.F. Stirm Brewery	Payette	1890–1891
California Brewery & Bakery	Pioneer City	1865
City Brewery	Pioneer City	1865
Pioneer Brewery	Pioneer City	1867–1869
W.A. Nunnally Brewery	Pioneer City	1871
Jos. Stadtmillier Brewery	Pioneer City	1874–1880
Boise Brewery	Placerville	1864–1867
Weldon & Kohny Brewery	Placerville	1869
Boise Brewery	Placerville	1874–1888
American Brewing Company	Pocatello	1902–1904
Franklin & Hayes Brewing Company	Pocatello	1904–1913
East Idaho Brewing Company Inc.	Pocatello	1935–1954
Henry Reiniger Brewery	Rathdrum	1881–1883
City Brewery	Rathdrum	1886–1889

Brewery Name	Location	Open Dates
Freitz Stabb Brewery	Rocky Bar	unknown–1870
Jacob Ulrich Brewery	Rocky Bar	1888–1890
Waymire & Waymire Brewery	Rocky Bar	1891–1896
Clarence H. Waymire Brewery	Rocky Bar	1897–1901
Edward Hosp & Company Brewery	Ruby City	1865
Schrader & Hosp Brewery	Ruby City	1866
Spahn & Deletraz Brewery	Salmon City	1867
Michael Spahn Brewery	Salmon City	1874–1897
X. Nutz Brewery	Salmon City	1886–1887
Spahn & Langendorf Brewery	Salmon City	1897–1898
Freda & Warnecke Brewery	Salmon City	1898–1899
William Warnecke Brewery	Salmon City	1899–1903
City Brewery	Shoshone	1886–1890
A. Grete & Bro. Brewery	Silver City	1866
Grete & Williams Brewery	Silver City	1866
Sommercamp & Bray Brewery	Silver City	1866–unknown
Williams & Slagle Brewery	Silver City	1866
A. Schrader & A. Hosp Brewery	Silver City	1867
Miners Brewery	Silver City	1867
Miners Brewery Saloon	Silver City	1867
Owyhee Bakery & Brewery	Silver City	1868
City Brewery	Silver City	1869
Star Brewery & Billiard Saloon	Silver City	1874–1884
Frederick Grete Sr. Brewery	Silver City	1888–1903
J.T. Hunt Brewery	Silver City	1890–1891
George Rambour Brewery	Silver City	1903–1904
Owyhee Brewery	Silver City	1903–1915
Largilliere & Schmidt Brewery	Soda Springs	1884

Brewery Name	Location	Open Dates
August Largilliere Brewery	Soda Springs	1884–1904
John Lemp Brewery	South Mountain	1875
Jos. Stadtmiller & Steward Brewery	Vienna	1882
Adelbert L. Rice Brewery	Victor	1898–1905
St. Anthony Brewing Company	St. Anthony	1901–1910
South Idaho Brewers Inc. Brewery	Twin Falls	1934
Carl Mallon Brewery	Wallace	1889–1902
Sunset Brewing Company	Wallace	1901–1915
Sunset Mercantile Company Inc. Brewery	Wallace	1934–1937
Sunset Brewing Company	Wallace	1937–1939
Sunset Mercantile Company Brewery	Wallace	1939–1946
Deluxe Brewing Company	Wallace	1946
Otto Arnold Brewery	Wardner	1886–1887
Scott & Lingley Brewery	Wardner	1888
South Fork Brewery	Wardner	1888–1893
Geo. Gleim Brewery	Wardner	1890–1896
Joseph Faul Brewery	Wardner	1894
J.J. Manuel Brewery	Warren's Diggings	1866
Raymond Saux Brewery	Washington	1874–1875
John O. Peters Brewery	Weiser	1884–1886
Sylvester Werneth Brewery	Weiser	1886–1890
Mrs. Sylvester Werneth Brewery	Weiser	1891–1902
Gus Fleigner Brewery	Weiser	1902–1906

IDAHO BREWERIES OPENING IN 2014

BREWERY	CITY	BREWERS
Black Bird Brewing	Boise	Shane Gibbs
Bogus Brewing	Boise	Collin Rudeen, Lance Chavez
Cloud Nine	Boise	Jake Lake
Edge Brewing	Boise	Kerry Caldwell
Powderhaus	Boise	Tyson Cardon
Woodland Empire Ale Craft	Boise	Rob Landerman
Mad Bomber Brewing	Hayden	Tom Applegate
Accomplice Brewing	Meridian	Tim Williams
County Line Brewery	Meridian	Zack Kiehl
Haff Brewing	Meridian	Brian Haff
Simian Brewing	Nampa	Marvin Kinny

INDEX

ABOUT THE AUTHOR

S teven Koonce (@thedailybeard on Twitter, @thedailybeard on Untappd) has been a craft beer fan since discovering Stone Brewing in 2003 and has been an avid home-brewer for more than a decade. Steven graduated with honors with a degree in film production from Chapman University in 2001. He writes the Idaho On Tap beer blog for magicvalley.com in Twin Falls, where he lives with his fiancée, Valerie; her two children, Cameron and Lily; and his two dogs, Prudence and Nabisco.

His hobbies include hiking, fishing, golfing and cheering on his beloved Seahawks, Mariners and University of Washington Huskies. He owns and operates a video production company called Like Button, and he creates high-quality commercial and long-form videos for clients around southern Idaho.

Besides beer, Steven enjoys fine food, red wine and Kentucky bourbon. His favorite non-Idaho beer is Stone IPA. Among his favorite Idaho beers are Laughing Dog's the Dogfather Imperial Stout, Payette Outlaw IPA and Infidel from Selkirk Abbey. Additionally, Dagger Falls IPA is almost always in his refrigerator.

Visit us at
www.historypress.net
....
This title is also available as an e-book